I0192591

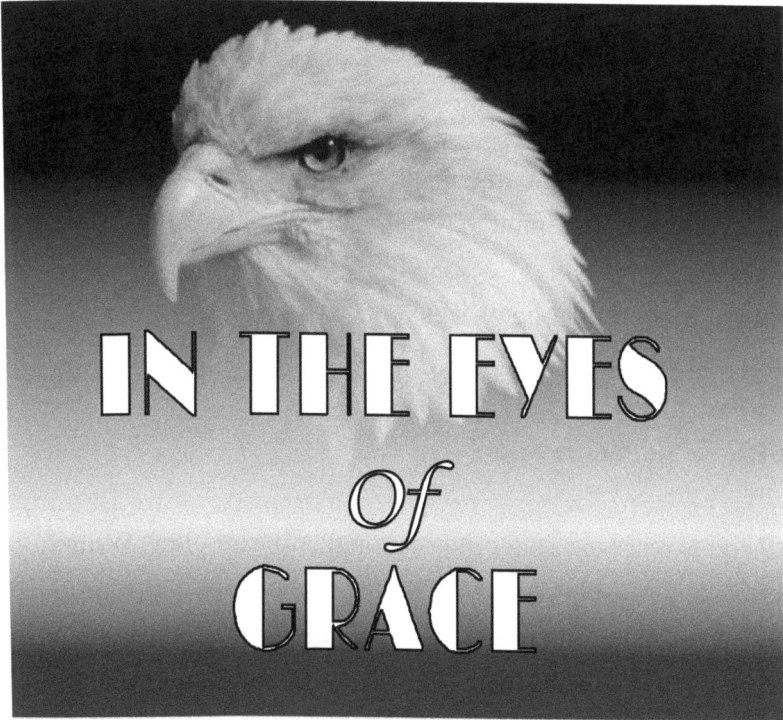

# IN THE EYES Of GRACE

Unveiling Truth as God sees

## Pst. Bonface E. Odhiambo

IN THE EYES OF GRACE
Copyright @2014 by Pastor Bonface Odhiambo

P. O. Box 28831- 00200
City Square, Nairobi
Tel: +254 721664587
Email: bonfireod@gmail.com
website: www.gracefamilychapel.net

Printed in the Republic of Kenya
First edition 2014

ISBN: 978-9966-069-04-7

All rights reserved under international copyright law. Written permission must be secured from the author to use or reproduce any part of this book either electronically or manually except for brief quotations in critical reviews or articles. Bible questions unless otherwise indicated are from New King James version (NKJV) of the Holy Bible, copyright @ 1982 used by permission of Thomas Nelson Publishers, 1982 all rights reserved.

Acknowledgments
First and foremost I give glory and honor to the almighty God who directed me into these truths and inspired this writing. He gave me the courage to put down these truths to influence many lives.

I wish to thank my family especially my wife Jacqueline who gave me support and encouraged me to write. I also express my gratitude to Francois du Toit and the mirrorword team who introduced me to this realm of truth. I cannot forget to appreciate Grace Abundant Family Chapel members who were patient with me to teach these truths to them and the Grace Ministers Alliance who have supported me and believed in me. My friend Pastor Maurice Mwale and the entire family of Grace Covenant Church who never ceased to encourage me. Also EvPs. John and Debby Fair of Miracle Life Ministries who have consistently been an encouragement to me and all friends who supported me and believed in me. May the Lord greatly reward you. I greatly value all your input in my life.

## Foreword by Francois du Toit

Pst Bonface's book, In The Eyes Of Grace is a celebration of God's love for you.

The gospel reveals the love initiative of God; our sins did not distract from His extravagant love for humanity!

Through the pages of this study, chapter after chapter you will hear the echo of Pst Bonface's passion, just like Paul who wrote (Ephesians 3:9) "I want to make all mankind see!"

The simplicity of the gospel is also its dynamic! The only belief that matters, is what God believes! Jesus is what God believes! The faith of God has conquered the odds! One has died for all! Therefore all have died! Just as it was appointed for man to die once and then face judgment, so Jesus died once and faced our judgment! Never to deal with sin again, but to reveal salvation! (Rom 1:16,17, 2 Cor 5:14-21, Heb 9:27,28)

None of the wise rulers of this age understood the simplicity of this mystery! In God's economy, Jesus represents the human race! Without our permission or contribution, God singlehandedly wrought our deliverance from the powers of death and hell!

This book will awaken the life of the ages within you! The joyful adventure to bless the nations with the grandest announcement ever! Glad tidings of great joy that belongs to the human race!

The world is waiting to hear this life awakening message!

## DEDICATION.

This book is dedicated to my late mother Reginah Auma Odhiambo. Through her godly character she shaped our lives by introducing us to church at an early age. She committed her life to the church as long as we knew her and saw to it that her family followed her steps. Though she is gone but what she shaped in me still remains. We will live to remember you.

# PREFACE

I thank my heavenly Father for His love and grace to us, the Father has chosen to reveal Himself to us in His grace through Jesus Christ our Lord. All that can be known about Him has been revealed but the enemy has taken advantage to keep the church in the dark about who our God is and what He has accomplished for us. Just as in the parable of the ten virgins, they all looked alike waiting for the groom. But five of them were in the dark, they could hear but could not see, they needed illumination of the Spirit to see. Today we face the same dilemma, many of us in the church are still in the dark and as Paul prayed that we all may see, that is the prayer that led to the writing of this book. That we may see the finished work of Christ and cease from our own labor.

Truth has the capacity to set free, truth is like a lion, you need not find a prey for it, only set it free and it will find its own prey. This truth is meant to find its own prey and bring real liberation to the lives of many. A man lights a spotlight on a sunny day, the spotlight seems not effective at all though it is light. The sun seems more superior to the spotlight, it is a higher light than the spotlight and carries more authority. In the same manner we have lesser truths and higher truth. This is to help you see truth in a higher level for transformation of lives. The questions you have often asked yourself weather God is Love and why then does He seem far from us, what are the implication of the cross to the human race and the life of a believer today?

This book goes to a greater length to bring to clarity the finished work of Christ on the cross. Its purpose is for us to enjoy every blessing that God has purposed for us and paid the price for us to enjoy, the free gifts God has bestowed on us. To understand our completeness and cease from entertaining religion in our thoughts. It's a call for the church to come out of the religious box we have found ourselves in and think of life full of liberty. A life which God purposed for us to live free from guilt and condemnation. A life of God, partakers of divine nature. As you read through the pages of this book, know that this is what God has intended for you all this long but the enemy has kept you in the dark. The revelation of God's grace is what you need.

As you peer through the pages of this book, let your heart be inspired, your eyes be enlightened and your mind be transformed by this truth. Let the reality of the cross dawn on you and let every shade of darkness be expelled from your understanding by the light of the Word. Let a fresh fountain flow from within you and let tears of joy roll down your cheeks as you discover a life of real freedom. Freedom which we often speak of but we rarely experience. Let this be the dawning of a new life to you fresh and separate from the religious gimmicks you have subjected your life.

Pst. Bonface Odhiambo.

# CONTENTS

*All Scripture unless otherwise indicated are from New King James Version* (Thomas Nelson Publishers, 1982) With bold emphasis.

# *ONE*

## THE NATURE OF GOD

*"God, who at various times and in various ways spoke in time past to the fathers by the prophets, has in these last days spoken to us by His Son, whom He has appointed heir of all things, through whom also He made the worlds; who being the brightness of His glory and the express image of His person, and upholding all things by the word of His power, when He had by Himself purged our sins, sat down at the right hand of the Majesty on high,"* (Heb 1:1-3).

God has in these last days manifested Himself through Jesus Christ. The Son is the exact representation of the Father, He manifests the Father in every aspect of His being. We have been struggling in our religion about the character of God and most often we have borrowed what we see happening under the law as the true manifestation of the nature of the Father.

When the Son walked physically in this earth, everything He did was the exact representation of the character of the Father, He Himself testified, ...., *"Most assuredly, I say to you, the Son can do nothing of Himself, but what He sees the Father do; for whatever He does, the Son also does in like manner. "For the Father loves the Son, and shows Him all things that He Himself does; and He will show Him greater works than these, that you may marvel."For as the Father raises the dead and gives life to them, even so the Son gives life to whom He will.* " (John 5:19-21). The Father raises the dead and gives them life, He does not kill and bring diseases.

The Son likewise raises the dead and gives life, He heals all oppressed, the sick and above all He took upon Himself all our sicknesses on His body on the cross (Math 8:17). Everything we saw the Son doing in His physical earthly ministry manifests the true character of what the Father is and what He intended for man from the beginning.

*"How God anointed Jesus of Nazareth with the Holy Spirit and with power, who went about doing good and healing all who were oppressed by the devil, for God was with Him."*(Acts 10:38). Jesus went about doing good and healing all who were oppressed, the nature of God is good and God desires goodness for His people, He is not the author of diseases and if He was, then Christ went against His will by healing all who were oppressed by demons. Brothers it will be wrong for us to preach a God who brings curses when His own Son went through all that pain on that cross to take away curses, was that suffering only a formality? Was it not meant for our freedom from curses? How can we continue preaching a God of curses after He has gone all this length to set us free? *"For this purpose the Son of God was manifested, that he might destroy the works of the devil."* (1 John 3:8)

As the character of the Father is good so the Son went about doing good and destroyed all that was of the devil. That is what God has revealed about Himself, any other knowledge of God apart from this is not of God, but from the devil.

*"And Then God saw everything that He had made, and indeed it was very good. So the evening and the morning were the sixth day,"* (Gen 1:31). When God finished His creative work everything He created was good, nothing bad and contrary to His intentions for man and for the earth had He created, He included gold, bdellium and onyx stones in the garden of Eden. Only at one instance did He say *"it is not good,"* when He saw man alone without a companion. Since the time of creation, His intent for man has always been good and hasn't changed nor is He about to change. James confidently affirms to the goodness of our God. *"Every desirable and beneficial gift comes out of heaven. The gifts are rivers of light cascading down from the Father of Light. **There is nothing deceitful in God, nothing two-faced, nothing fickle."*** (James 1:17, Message). He is not about to change from this and wants you to be aware of this.

The more we study the Bible the more we are left with questions which need answers, the problem has not been God but the understanding we have carried about God. We have known God from a law mentality and missed the opportunity of enjoying His embrace in our lives. *"Now Cain talked with Abel his brother; and it came to pass, when they were in the field, that Cain rose up against Abel his brother and killed him. Then the LORD said to Cain, "Where is Abel your brother?" He said, "I do not know. Am I my brother's keeper?" And He said, "What have you done? The voice of your brother's blood cries out to Me from the ground. "So now you are cursed from the earth, which has opened its mouth to receive your brother's blood from your hand. "When you till the ground, it shall no longer yield its strength to you. A fugitive and a vagabond you shall be on the earth." And Cain said to the LORD, "My punishment is greater than I can bear! "Surely You have driven me out this day from the face of the ground; I shall be hidden from Your face; I shall be a fugitive and a vagabond on the earth, and it will happen that anyone who finds me will kill me." And the LORD said to him, "Therefore, whoever kills Cain, vengeance shall be taken on him sevenfold." And the LORD set a mark on Cain, lest anyone finding him should kill him. Then Cain went out from the presence of the LORD and dwelt in the land of Nod on the east of Eden." (Gen 4:8-16)*

Cain boldly answers God "Am I my brothers keeper?" Where does this man Cain get such boldness to answer God? Is there something he knew about God that we have failed to know? I tend to believe Cain had numerous encounters with God that He was no longer a mystery to him but a buddy he knew well, even after God gave him a sentence for what he had done, he boldly complains of his punishment. God vows to protect him. Cain knew of the loving nature of God, even when he was guilty of committing an offence, he was sure he will get an audience with God.

The fall of man did not separate God from man, separation is an illusion, all things consist in Him, in Him we live, move and have our being (Acts 17:24), it's man who has been running away from God, we were separated in our minds from God. Jesus did not come to reconcile God back to man, God was in Christ reconciling the world back to Himself not imputing their sins on them. (2 Cor 5:19). God drove Adam out of Eden to protect him from eating the tree of life so that he may not live forever in a fallen state, He continually had conversations with Adam and that's why Adam's offspring come to appreciate God by offering sacrifices to Him. Cain discovered the loving nature of God and God vows to protect the first murderer. That's the nature of my God. *"For his anger lasts only a moment, but his favor lasts a lifetime!"* (Ps 30:5a, NLT) Wow that's the God you ought to discover, the message translation brings it much stronger, *"**He gets angry once in a while, but across a lifetime there is only love.**"*

## Generations.

To fully view the picture the Bible portrays about the nature of our God, we have to look at all generations the Bible speaks of. In every generation the loving kindness of God is displayed to a people who never qualified to be loved or favored. Enoch walks with God until he is no more in the midst of wickedness. Noah and his family found grace when the entire world was involved in violence. God picked him up and reveals Himself to Noah, he found favor in the eyes of God, (Gen 6:8). God picks Abraham in a society of idolaters, Abraham was not better than the others but God chose to reveal Himself to Abraham and makes him a father of many. Lot is rescued by the angel of God before the destruction of Sodom, his family found favor in God's eyes.

Jacob was not perfect to be chosen by God over Esau, he was a trickster yet God chose him. Abraham his grand father lied before a gentile king, so did Isaac yet God still identified Himself with

5

them. Judah has a son by his daughter in-law, a gentile woman Tamar who becomes part of the genealogy of Christ. Their son Perez was one of the ancestors of Christ. (Gen 38:16-), Joseph a type of Christ who was faultless marries a gentile woman Asenath the daughter of Portiphera the priest of On. The type of Christ marrying the gentile Church, (Gen 48:14). Jacob blesses Ephraim over Manasseh the first born of Joseph, God's unconditional choice, Ephraim never deserved this yet he received the blessing of the first born. Gentiles never deserved it but we have received the blessing of son-ship.

God picks Moses a murderer to be a deliverer of His people from Egypt. Moses by all standards was not qualified, he was a murderer on the run from Egypt, married to a gentile, not eloquent in speech but God chose him. Israel deliverance from Egypt was not because they were righteous, two months out of the land of Egypt they curved an idol and worshiped it. This is what they used to do in Egypt. They were delivered because of Abraham's covenant with God, and that's how we also today are saved through Christ's covenant with God.

**Rahab a gentile prostitute from Jericho finds her name in the genealogy of Christ**, same to Ruth a Moabite (gentile) and Bathsheba a gentile woman and wife to King David. (Matt 1:5-6). David was chosen and anointed to be king at a very tender age, there were many in the tribe of Judah who felt more qualified to be king than David but David a young shepherd boy was chosen. When David killed Uriah and took his wife, God did not deal with him according to the Law of Moses, otherwise he deserved to die.

Solomon married many gentile women and fell into idolatry but was never punished for all these, he walked under the covenant God made with David. Same to us today we enjoy the blessing of the covenant secured to us by Jesus Christ. Daniel, Esther, Nehemiah and many more received divine favor in foreign lands.

The nation of Israel was preserved many times when they fell into idolatry; they were never wiped out as some nations were. As we look at the big picture, we see a loving God who favored people who completely never deserved to be favored. A man once wrote a book how he changed his faith from Christianity to Islam because most of the heroes in the Bible had tainted characters. This is what religion does, it demands perfection but can't lift a finger to help you attain perfection. God chose people not because they qualified but because of His love and qualified them. If it was only one or two cases, we could easily dismiss these as exceptions but it is something which is continually repeated, this is the true nature of God. We can not define God by few exceptional cases where wrath is revealed in accordance to the demands of the law.

Ezekiel describes the relationship which God had with Israel, *"on the day you were born, no one cared about you. Your umbilical cord was not cut, and you were never washed, rubbed with salt, and wrapped in cloth. No one had the slightest interest in you; no one pitied you or cared for you. On the day you were born, you were unwanted, dumped in a field and left to die. "But I came by and saw you there, helplessly kicking about in your own blood. As you lay there, I said, 'Live!' And I helped you to thrive like a plant in the field. You grew up and became a beautiful jewel.*

*Your breasts became full, and your body hair grew, but you were still naked. And when I passed by again, I saw that you were old enough for love. So I wrapped my cloak around you to cover your nakedness and declared my marriage vows. I made a covenant with you, says the Sovereign LORD, and you became mine. "Then I bathed you and washed off your blood, and I rubbed fragrant oils into your skin. I gave you expensive clothing of fine linen and silk, beautifully embroidered, and sandals made of fine goatskin leather. I gave you lovely jewelry, bracelets, beautiful necklaces, a ring for your nose, earrings for your ears, and a lovely crown for your head. And so you were adorned with gold and silver. Your clothes were made of fine linen and were beautifully embroidered. You ate the finest foods—choice flour, honey, and olive oil—and became more beautiful than ever. You looked like a queen, and so you were! Your fame soon spread throughout the world because of your beauty. I dressed you in my splendor and perfected your beauty, says the Sovereign LORD."* (Eze. 16:4-14, NLT)

Ezekiel paints a picture of a loving God who chose Israel from nothing, took care of her, beautified her and made a covenant of love with her, Israel did not continue in this covenant but God's love for Israel remained steadfast. That's how much the Father has always loved us; our behavior has never changed His love from you. He picked us when none could admire us, washed us in His blood, clothed us in His righteousness, beautified us with gifts of His Spirit, made us sons, He has done to us what we never deserved because of His love for us. *"For God so loved the world that He gave His one and only son that whoever believes in Him should not perish but have eternal life,"* (Jn 3:16). **God loved the world in its fallen state,** He never waited for the world to reform first, change its character before loving us, we never repented first before He poured His love to us. Even creation itself was inspired by love. A loving God had to create a being to express His love to. Love can not exist in isolation, it must be manifested. We were created to experience love and man has no ability to resist love. **God has not wasted His love on man but invested it on man.** David discovers the loving kindness of God when he was fleeing from his son Absalom, (Psalms 63:3-5).

> *"Because Your loving-kindness is better than life, My lips shall praise You. Thus I will bless You while I live; I will lift up my hands in Your name. My soul shall be satisfied as with marrow and fatness, and my mouth shall praise You with joyful lips."*

David discovered that God's loving kindness is more than life. Though he was guilty of the murder of Uriah, he understood that the loving kindness of God surpasses every offence he had committed. (God's loving kindness is in plenty supply more than life). You can't spend one day without seeing God's love in plenty expressed on us. If you have faith to see another day then you need very little faith to see God's goodness manifested to you, it's in plenty supply more than life. **Right belief results in right living.** When we fill our minds with doubts about God, we will live in fear. Any meaningful friendship must be void of suspicion; it must be based on absolute trust.

### Plague of Sin.
There are some excepts in the Old Testament where it is recorded how God wiped out cities, nations and the entire generation.

9

*"Then the LORD saw that the wickedness of man was great in the earth, and that every intent of the thoughts of his heart was only evil continually. And the LORD was sorry that He had made man on the earth, and He was grieved in His heart. So the LORD said, "I will destroy man whom I have created from the face of the earth, both man and beast, creeping thing and birds of the air, for I am sorry that I have made them." But Noah found grace in the eyes of the LORD. "* (Gen 6:5-8)

Sin threatened the promise of God, the devils purpose was to corrupt the seed of the woman. God had promised that the Messiah would come through the seed of the woman (Gen 3:15). When sin matures it brings forth death. God had to protect the uncorrupted seed through Noah and his family. He obtained favor in God's eyes and the promises of God were fulfilled through his descendants. Since the fall of Adam there was sin in the world but sin is not accounted for where there is no law. *"Certainly sin was in the world before the law was given, but no record of sin is kept when there is no law."* (Rom 5:13, ISV)

Man was not aware of his sinfulness since there was no law to reveal sin. Sin was like a plague which threatened to wipe away the entire human generation, the Lamb of God who takes away the sins of the world had not been revealed. Sin reigned and brought death. This is why the nations which gave themselves to idolatry and demon worship were destroyed. When sin reigns it brings forth death. Israel was protected and mankind was also protected from being completely corrupted by sin. The promise of a messiah was kept alive and finally sin was given a final blow through the Messiah. God did not create man for destruction but to show him love and affection.

### The Lord's Identity.

Moses had a unique encounter with God, Israel had sinned by worshiping a golden calf, Moses went to intercede for them. And he said, *"Please, show me Your glory." Then He said, "I will make all My goodness pass before you, and I will proclaim the name of the LORD before you. I will be gracious to whom I will be gracious, and I will have compassion on whom I will have compassion."* (Exo 33:18-19)

Moses asks God to show him His glory, the Lord replies He will make His goodness pass before Moses. God does not show His wrath but His goodness, He is ready to reveal goodness to us at any moment. (His glory is about His goodness), **when God appears, only goodness manifests**. The Lord will proclaim His name, His identity before Moses. His name reveals His identity. He will be gracious to whom He wishes and show compassion to whom He wishes. Grace and compassion that's what God wishes to show to whoever He chooses not wrath not anger. And the good news is, through Christ Jesus, God has shown His grace and compassion upon all mankind.

*"And the LORD passed before him and proclaimed, "The LORD, the LORD God, merciful and gracious, longsuffering, and abounding in goodness and truth, "keeping mercy for thousands, forgiving iniquity and transgression and sin, by no means clearing the guilty, visiting the iniquity of the fathers upon the*

*children and the children's children to the third and the fourth generation." So Moses made haste and bowed his head toward the earth, and worshiped."* (Exo 34:6-8).

The Lord revealed Himself to Moses as a merciful God, full of grace and longsuffering (patience), full of goodness and truth, keeping mercy for thousands, other versions say keeping mercy for a thousand generation, forgiving iniquity, transgression and sin. By no means clearing the guilty. He ensures the guilty are punished. How did God ensure the guilty are punished? By initiating the sacrificial system where the guilty could transfer their sin and guilt to an animal and that animal bore their guilt and sin and died with it. **The sacrificial system ensured the lamb bore the sin and guilt of the sinner.**

The sacrificial system pointed to the coming of Christ who was the lamb of God that takes away our sins. John calls Him the lamb of God who takes away the sin of the world (John 1:29). God in His fore knowledge understood the existence of sin in the future and set apart Christ to be the lamb who would deal with sins of men, (1 Pet 1:18-20). This is grace at its best that God ensured the guilty will always go free through the sacrificial system. A God who clears the guilty, who can do this if not Jehovah? The world which stood condemned has been redeemed and restored to innocence.

In the sacrificial system, the sinner was never examined but the lamb was examined, it had to be blameless. The blameless life of the lamb was not important to God but to the sinner. The lamb took the sin of the sinner and died with it, the sinner took the blameless life of the lamb and went free. There was no more fear of judgment on him and he was fully reconciled to his maker. This is exactly what the perfect sacrifice of Christ accomplished. Man who was guilty was acquitted, reconciled to God and man only needs to believe. He never sent an angel to bear the punishment but become the lamb Himself.

Visiting the iniquity of the fathers on their children to the fourth generation. How did He visit their iniquity? By mercy, mercy is not for the innocent but for the guilty. A God who is full of mercy and grace, forgiving iniquity, transgression and sin is not a God to be feared or dreaded but to be worshiped. He has given us an option of forgiving our sins and showing mercy and grace. Mercy is not being given what you deserve especially when you are wrong, Grace is getting good that which you never deserved. Once our sins are forgiven, we don't have to worry that our children will bear our sins. His mercies endure for a thousand generation, which means even in the fourth generation His mercy is still available. We have no excuse to live in poverty when someone has deposited ten million dollars in our account.

When David counted the fighting men and was asked in whose hands he would wish to fall, he chose to fall in the hands of God because His mercies are great. Had he chosen to fall by the hand of man, maybe he could have died. (1 Chron. 21:13). Mercy triumphs over judgment (James 2:3). When Moses heard this, he worshiped God and found the courage to ask God to go with them which had been difficult earlier. He discovered the soft spot of

God. Then he said, "*If now I have found grace in Your sight, O Lord, let my Lord, I pray, go among us, even though we are a stiff–necked people; and pardon our iniquity and our sin, and take us as Your inheritance.*" (Exo 34:9). After Moses knew who God is, he quickly took advantage and asked God to accompany them, to forgive their sin and take them as His inheritance.

That is what we need to know about our God, He never revealed Himself as a God of wrath and anger. In numbers 14, Israel sinned against God by believing the bad report from the ten spies, God was angry and Moses quickly takes advantage of what he knew about God and intercedes for Israel.

'*The LORD is longsuffering and abundant in mercy, forgiving iniquity and transgression; but He by no means clears the guilty, visiting the iniquity of the fathers on the children to the third and fourth generation.*' "*Pardon the iniquity of this people, I pray, according to the greatness of Your mercy, just as You have forgiven this people, from Egypt even until now.*" *Then the LORD said: "I have pardoned, according to your word; Vs 18-20.* According to the greatness of God's mercy He pardoned them. They failed to reach the promised land not because God refused but because they said it themselves (Vs 28). They said their carcass will fall in the wilderness and that's what they got. God did not transfer their sins to their children; He forgave their sins and let their children enter the land of promise, but the people chose to die in the wilderness by employing unbelief. Unbelief has no remedy; they failed to enter because of unbelief. In the same manner redemption is complete, man has to believe on the finished work, Grace at His best. We always claim we are preaching grace, we are saved by grace but end up preaching a harsh God who is at war with man. Grace is not for the qualified but for the unqualified, not for the deserving but undeserving. If we preach a gracious God then grace should be from start to end. We were unqualified but now qualified. Grace means grace and nothing less. Grace has come and grace is Christ Himself, *"of His fullness have we all received grace upon grace,"* (John 1:16).

Abraham had failed to take advantage of the mercies of God when he was interceding for Sodom. The Lord visited Abraham to inform him what was happening in Sodom, Sodom and the entire region belonged to Abraham. God had told him as far as his eyes could see He would give to Him. Before going to Sodom He had to let Abraham know. Abraham only insisted on getting ten righteous, had he continued until one righteous person, definitely the city could have been spared for the sake of Lot and his family. Abraham could have relied on God's character and insisted on forgiveness (Gen 18:23-33). Remember all these happened before the cross, all the mercy they enjoyed was pointing to the coming of Christ. Now we are not dealing with God who is out to pour His anger and wrath, His anger against sin was swallowed up at the cross, He pours out grace on us.

### Comes the Law

Abraham the friend of God and patriarch from whose lineage the Messiah comes marries his sister. *"And Abraham said, "Because I thought, surely the fear of God is not in this place; and they will kill me on account of my wife. But indeed she is truly my sister.*

15

*"She is the daughter of my father, but not the daughter of my mother, and she became my wife." (Gen 20:11-12)*. He marries his step sister, same father but different mothers. After the law is given in (Lev 18), any person who does that was to be stoned to death. Jacob marries two sisters of the same father, an act which is punishable by stoning (Lev 18). God revealed Himself to Jacob, blessed him and even protected him from his enemies. His nature towards man has always been loving.

The system of the law disqualified people who God qualified. The law is a system which was added because of transgression, it's a system which came in to make man discover sin. This system had an authority behind it which ensured it was adhered to and enforced. Gal 3:19 tells us the angels ordained this system through Moses. This system does not know forgiveness, or mercy or grace contrary to God's nature. It demands punishment to every violation. The law does not in any way portray the nature of a loving, caring, merciful, gracious and forgiving God. Lets separate the two and embrace the God of love, He is not schizophrenic. If sin were greater than His love then redemption could be impossible.

After God finished His work of creation He rested on the seventh day, He saw Himself in man whom He had made in His image and likeness, just as a master artist finishes his masterpiece and rests because he sees what he had in mind portrayed on the surface. 'the first Hebrew word in Genesis, *bereshet*, from *be*, in and *rosh*, head, means "in the head," you are His inspired thought, the original thought.'[1]

*1, Francois du Toit 'God believes in you. pg 22'*

We are the expression of God. Mankind is the God kind. We are the carriers of the image and likeness of God. (When God designed you He had no other reference but Himself, **He looked at Himself to design you)**. He is not confused about you. A compass, a man made device cannot be confused of the north direction no matter where you take it, what about our God the maker of all heaven and earth? How can He be confused about you? He has never turned His mind against man since the fall of Adam. How can He forget about you? Even after the fall of Adam, God did not renegotiate the price to pay to redeem man, He never said " you know, man has been corrupted by sin for 4000 years so his value has reduced." No, He paid the full price for man.

We often sing some religious songs asking God to remember us as if God suffers from amnesia. **To forget you is to forget Himself**. *"who is man that thou are mindful of him....,* (Psalms 8:4). God's mind is full of thoughts of you, to forget you will simply mean He has lost His mind. *"And Your thoughts toward us Cannot be recounted to You in order; If I would declare and speak of them, They are more than can be numbered, "*(Psalms 40:5).

*"How precious also are Your thoughts to me, O God! How great is the sum of them! If I should count them, they would be more in number than the sand; When I awake, I am still with You."* (Psalms 139:17-18). Job discovered God could not turn His eye from him even for a second. *"What is man, that You should exalt him, That **You should set Your heart on him**, That You should visit him every morning......? How long? **Will You not look away***

17

*from me, And let me alone till I swallow my saliva?"*
(Job 7:17-19). These men lived before the cross yet they had such
understanding of God, but to us whom God has made residence in
us we still struggle with such truth. Religion has reduced us to
begging, begging for the presence of God and His attention yet
He promised never to leave us nor forsake us unconditionally,
(Heb 13:8). Does this sound familiar to you or foreign, you need
to understand the one who loves you.

## Goodwill
Luke 2:8-14
*"Now there were in the same country shepherds living out in the
fields, keeping watch over their flock by night. And behold, an
angel of the Lord stood before them, and the glory of the Lord
shone around them, and they were greatly afraid. Then the angel
said to them, "Do not be afraid, for behold, I bring you good
tidings of great joy which will be to all people. "For there is born
to you this day in the city of David a Savior, who is Christ the Lord.
"And this will be the sign to you: You will find a Babe wrapped in
swaddling cloths, lying in a manger." And suddenly there was
with the angel a multitude of the heavenly host praising God and
saying: "Glory to God in the highest, And on earth peace,
goodwill toward men!"*

When Christ was born, the message the angels brought was good
news to all the people. Good news is only good if you are included
in it, all mankind was included in this report. The angels
proclaimed peace and goodwill towards all men. God has
declared peace to all mankind, He is not at war with us, He has

reconciled Himself to us. Reconciliation was not our initiative, no; it has always been in His mind. Religion still portrays God who is at war with His creation. Remember the cross, that's the real picture, His purpose has clearly been portrayed through the cross, everything has changed in our favor. His plans for humanity are not at stake, nothing has jeopardized His purpose and intents for man. He found us in Christ before we fell in Adam. He has expressed goodwill to man. **Goodwill simply means good intentions to us.** He cannot proclaim goodwill to us and give us the opposite. We should arm our minds with this understanding.

Christ revealed the clear intentions of the Father by doing all He did while He walked on our planet. We cannot expect what is contrary to good from our God. *"Now it came to pass, when the time had come for Him to be received up, that He steadfastly set His face to go to Jerusalem, and sent messengers before His face. And as they went, they entered a village of the Samaritans, to prepare for Him. But they did not receive Him, because His face was set for the journey to Jerusalem. And when His disciples James and John saw this, they said, "Lord, do You want us to command fire to come down from heaven and consume them, just as Elijah did?" But He turned and rebuked them, and said, "You do not know what manner of spirit you are of. "For the Son of Man did not come to destroy men's lives but to save them." And they went to another village."* (Luke 9:51-56)

Jesus is rejected in the Samaritan village, the first thought which comes in the mind of James and John sons of thunder was to call fire from heaven to consume the city for rejecting the Messiah, the son of God who has come to give them the good news and heal their sick. How could they reject Him, how? But Jesus rebukes them, they were of a contrary spirit than love. If it was God's will to destroy man, then that was the right opportunity for fire to come from heaven and consume that village. Jesus come to seek and save, He humbly left the city for another day. When Elijah called fire from heaven and destroyed the soldiers who came to arrest him, he used the authority given to him as a prophet of God. He did not ask for permission from God. Some things we do and assume it is the will of God, but very contrary to what God wishes for us. Remember he was under the other covenant.

You have no reason to spend another day not sure of what to expect from Him, **ignorance empowers an already defeated enemy.** The devil takes advantage and fills our minds with all kinds of lies about God. (Mathew 25: 14-30), The parable of a master and his servants, the reason the servant with one talent hid his was: -( vs. 24-27) *"Then he who had received the one talent came and said, 'Lord, I knew you to be a hard man, reaping where you have not sown, and gathering where you have not scattered seed. 'And I was afraid, and went and hid your talent in the ground. Look, there you have what is yours.' "But his lord answered and said to Him, 'You wicked and lazy servant, you knew that I reap where I have not sown, and gather where I have not scattered seed. 'So you ought to have deposited my money with the bankers, and at my coming I would have received back my own with interest."*

Negative attitude about his master was the reason he never invested. He knew his master to be a hard man who reaps where he did not sow and gathers where he had not scattered. He hid his talent on the ground so his master will have nothing at his return. This is how God has been portrayed in our churches; a hard man who we have to pray so hard and for hours to get His attention. To spend days in fasting to change His mind about us, we have to plant seeds so He can bless us and if we do not, no blessings. When we fail to give, He pours curses to us. God who has to pass us through hard times to teach us? No. No wonder the believers are struggling and many are giving up on this walk of faith. After many years of struggle with these teachings it only filled my heart with fear. I prayed not because I enjoyed prayer but because I feared punishment. I fasted not to miss heaven and I gave not because I loved to give but I feared curses. Hostility is the greatest distance that keeps people apart more than time or distance. We have created a hostile God in our minds. Religion thrives on the basis of a harsh God who is not happy and therefore we must do our best to make Him happy, and get a priest to appease Him. God loves a cheerful giver not a fearful giver.

Life was not enjoyable at all under religion. If hard times was the best teacher then Somali should be the leading nation in sending out missionaries to the nations because they have endured hardship for a long time. The great tribulation believers will be much better than us because of the sufferings they will go through. God should have given apostles, prophets, evangelists, teachers, pastors and hard times. The Holy Spirit is our teacher,

He teaches us by reminding us what we have freely received in Jesus Christ and this inspires us.

We are parents, we have kids, we don't teach them by taking a hot red iron and burning their bodies and tell them, son, you know I love you and this pain will teach you good lessons of life, no father does that. If we who are not perfect fathers can not do that why should we expect the perfect Father, the one who understands fatherhood better than all of us to do that? Surely God will not afflict you with cancer or accidents to teach you, which lesson will you learn after you are dead? Hard times will always come in life but it is not God who authors them, He will always give us a way out and turn that which was meant for evil to be of good.

I have a son and as a father who cares I always warn him not to play in dirty water, because in there, there are great risks of being infected with diseases. Suppose my son plays in dirty water or he just happens to be infected with a virus, I will not sit down and tell him "you know son this disease is teaching you lessons of life," no, I will work hard to see he is cured of the infection whether he made a mistake or he was accidentally infected. God does not afflict us with diseases but we live in a fallen world full of imperfect people and the devil who will not rest, will cause trouble in our lives. God is out there to see us out of these troubles as a loving Father, that's why He will lead us not into temptations but deliver us from evil.

When God put Adam and Eve in the garden of Eden, He told Adam not to eat the fruit of the tree of the knowledge of good and evil. He never wanted them to know evil but only good which they saw from God. At no time did God send the devil to go and tempt them. God did not plan the fall of man. God is not the author of evil neither does He tempt anyone with evil. When they fell He already worked out a remedy to restore man back to his original position. He does not plan your down fall at any time as a loving Father, rather He thinks good of you and always gets you out of trouble in this fallen world where evil is always present to oppose you. Paul Ellis says "If you relate to God on the basis of obligation and performance, then you will falsely interpret life's hardships and spiritual attacks as works of God. Instead of submitting in faith to the unconditional love of the Father and resisting the devil, your unbelief will lead you to submit to the devil and resist the one who loves you."[1]

The result of carrying a negative attitude about our God will cause us to operate under fear. Our giving, our prayer, our fellowship with Him will be governed by fear not love. Perfect love casts away fear and this is what God wants for you and me. *"And as we live in God, our love grows more perfect. So we will not be afraid on the day of judgment, but we can face him with confidence because we live like Jesus here in this world. Such love has no fear, because perfect love expels all fear. If we are afraid, it is for fear of punishment, and this shows that we have not fully experienced his perfect love."* (1John 4:17-18, NLT) When we fully experience His perfect love, fear of judgment will not be part of our lives. All our motivation will be out of love and not fear. We need to rest in the understanding of how God loves us, His love never fails. The master's intention in the parable was to profit the servants not himself. Everything God has given to us is for our profit not His; He never took away the talents from the faithful servant but added him more for his profit who had earned more. My fellow brothers, let us not be yoked with the mentality of the old. The cross has revealed it all, **Christ absorbed all anger against sin on that cross,** God used the very act of man's hatred and violence to save us. He chose to become a victim of our violence and through it saved us. There are no more curses left out for you. Christ become a curse on that cross and took away all curses from us, which other curse remains for us?

## Love

Paul understood the love of God, *"for the love of Christ constrains us; because we thus judge, that if one died for all, then were all dead:"* (2 Cor 5:14). It is not the fear of hell that constrained Paul to preach, he understood our inclusion in Christ. We should be moved by discovering the love of God and not fear of hell to preach the word. Fear is not a force but the absence of realized conscious Love. Love has loved us, *"and we have known and believed the love that God hath to us. God is love; and he that dwells in love dwells in God, and God in him."* (1 John 4:16). No scripture refers to God as Wrath but the Bible clearly defines Him as love. We preach more wrath than we preach love, we are more conscious of wrath than love. Paul paints to us a picture of what love is. *"Love is kind, patient, longsuffering, keeps no record of wrongs, envies not, seeks not her own, rejoices not in iniquity but in truth, bears all things, believes all things, hopes all things, endures all things and Love never fails. "* (1 Cor 13:4-). All these characteristics befit our God who is Love Himself. Keeps no record of wrongs, endures all things, bears all things and never fails. A God of this nature is the one who has loved you. That's why He declares (Heb 13:5) He will never leave us nor forsake us unconditionally. He loved us with His life. **You are the investment of God. You are what makes God rich. A man's heart will be where his treasure is,** (Matt 6:21). God's heart has always been on you. You are His treasure. He sees value in you.

You are the joy that was set before Him, *"Looking unto Jesus, the author and finisher of our faith, who for the joy that was set before Him endured the cross, despising the shame, and has sat down at the right hand of the throne of God."* (Heb 12:2). He looked at you and looked at the cross, He looked at you again and looked at the cross and decided to face the cross to have you. He'd rather die than live without you. Live with this understanding.

*"Again, the kingdom of heaven is like unto treasure hid in a field; the which when a man hath found, he hides, and for joy thereof goes and sells all that he hath, and buys that field. Again, the kingdom of heaven is like unto a merchant man, seeking goodly pearls: Who, when he had found one pearl of great price, went and sold all that he had, and bought it. "* (Matt 13:44-45)

You are the agricultural land which has more value than the harvest it produces (full of diamonds). God saw this treasure in you and could not resist giving up all He could to get you. You are the pearl of great value which the merchant could not resist but had to get. You have to celebrate the value God has seen in you and comprehend His love for you. John the apostle discovered how much Christ loved him and only in his own writings do we find the statement *"the disciple whom Jesus loved the most."*

*"Now there was leaning on Jesus' bosom one of his disciples, whom Jesus loved.* (John 21:20) *Then Peter, turning about, sees the disciple whom Jesus loved following; which also leaned on his breast at supper, and said, Lord, which is he that betrays thee?"* (John 13:23). Jesus loved all the disciples equally but John personalized this love to himself. Personalize His love to you and discover the loving nature of your God. He is not about to change, that's what will build our faith in God, Faith works by love (Gal 5:6). When we see His love towards us it ignites our faith, God Has bestowed His loving nature on us. We should explore this character and stop our religious mentality of seeing a God who is at war with us who we must work so hard to make happy. No, God celebrates you and at no moment will He be angry with you. His anger against sin was expressed at the cross and has promised- *"For this is like the waters of Noah to Me; For as I have sworn That the waters of Noah would no longer cover the earth, So have I sworn That I would not be angry with you, nor rebuke you."* (Isaiah 54:9).

We are not dealing with a God who is in a bad mood who we must work hard to persuade to change His mind towards us but we deal with God who has already made up His mind about His creation.

He has reconciled Himself to His creation. God is happy over you and is rejoicing over you. *"The LORD your God in your midst, The Mighty One, will save; He will rejoice over you with gladness, He will quiet you with His love, He will rejoice over you with singing."* (Zephaniah 3:17) He rejoices with singing over you, that's your God who has fallen in love with you. *"How amiable are your tabernacles....,"* (Ps 84:1). You are God's dwelling, amiable and made for His comfort and glory.

You are God's greatest dream. You are His desire. God believed in your salvation even before you heard the gospel. He prophesied your salvation. He had none to replace you, *"while we were yet sinners Christ died for us, the righteous for the unrighteous."* (Rom 5:8). Your redemption was not a second thought, it was the original thought of God from the beginning. The entire Bible is about Jesus and all about Jesus is about you. God can not express Himself through anything else apart from you. Jesus did not come to persuade an angry God to be nice towards mankind, **He came to persuade hostile humanity about the goodness of God**.

We have entered into a relationship were the greater serves the least. In this relationship it is God who has offered a sacrifice for us. It is Him who wipes our tears. It is Him who washes our feet and who comforts us. It is not us who seek Him but Him who came to seek and to save us. It is not us to pray to Him not to leave us, but Him who promised never to leave us nor forsake us. It is not us to invite Him in our meetings but Him who promised whenever two or three are gathered in His name He is there. It is not us to walk and knock at His door but Him who has left His house and is now standing at the door of our hearts knocking, whoever will hear His voice and open for Him, He will get in and dine with him. It is Him who calls us, redeemed us, justified us, sanctified us and glorified us, who is our shepherd, our teacher, our healer, our protector, our helper, our high priest, our intercessor and our advocate. **God who is at your service, greater is Him who serves.**

Paul writes to the Ephesians how God out of His own will, purpose and pleasure chose us and blessed us. *"Paul an apostle by the will of God....,"* (Eph 1:1), *"having predestined us unto the adoption of children by Jesus Christ to himself, according to the good pleasure of his will,"* (vs 5), *"having made known to us the mystery of his will according to his good pleasure which he hath purposed in himself,"* (vs 9), *"in whom we have obtained an inheritance, being predestinated according to the purpose of him who worketh all things after the counsel of his own will."* (Vs 11). It was not out of our good behavior or something we did that made Him be favorable to us. It was out of His own good will, pleasure and purpose. The father of the prodigal son was waiting daily for the return of his son. He longed for him and missed him, that's how God has been waiting for you, His love surpasses all you may imagine. Whose testimony will you believe? God's testimony is greater than mans' testimony, (1 John 5:9). See yourself in His light. You need to know even as you are known by the Father. *".....So shall I know even as I have always been known."* (1 Cor 13:12)

# TWO

## THE COVENANTS

Covenants formed the basis of relationships in the Bible, for us to understand the relationships the people in the Old Testament enjoyed with God it will be of great significance if we understood the covenants they operated under. Covenants were basically like constitutions that stipulated the rules of engagement between different parties. Covenants were common in the near east tradition, and the Bible coming from the background of the near eastern tradition adopted the common pattern of these treaties.

The Vassal treaties in those days were employed in the near eastern when a greater power (the Suzerain king) imposed certain conditions of vassaldom on a smaller state (the vassal) which would normally have been conquered by the more powerful state in battle. The treaty explained the reason for imposition and the nature of the conditions imposed on the smaller state, and also made certain provisions relating to the maintenance of the treaty.

The same type of treaty also seems to have been employed throughout the near east and there is evidence of its use in simpler form, in Mesopotamia as early as the third millennium and also in Egypt. The Hebrew word for covenant (tyrb *ber-eeth'*) simply implies 'a contract or an agreement of two parties.' The agreement was conditional with each partner having a role to play. God made covenants with His people long ago, and these were like contracts which His people had a part to play and God had a part to play

God tells Abraham, *"walk before me blameless that I may fulfill my covenant with you."* (Gen 17:2)

*"then he took the Book of the Covenant and read in the hearing of the people. And they said, "All that the LORD has said we will do, and be obedient."And Moses took the blood, sprinkled it on the people, and said, "This is the blood of the covenant which the LORD has made with you according to all these words."* (Exodus 24:7-8)

*"Now it shall come to pass, if you diligently obey the voice of the LORD your God, to observe carefully all His commandments which I command you today, that the LORD your God will set you high above all nations of the earth. "And all these blessings shall come upon you and overtake you, because you obey the voice of the LORD your God:"* (Deuteronomy 28:1-2)

**The covenant was conditional, the people had to keep their part and God had to keep His part of the covenant.** God basically intended to bless His people through entering into these agreements with them. Wherever they failed to keep their part of the agreement the results were the opposite of all that God had intended for them. These covenants were dependent on the peoples' behavior, they had to do all their best so as to sustain the covenants and receive the blessings intended.

*"But it shall come to pass, if thou wilt not hearken unto the voice of the LORD thy God, to observe to do all his commandments and his statutes which I command thee this day; that all these curses shall come upon thee, and overtake thee: "* (Deut 28:15)

When they failed to keep their part of the covenants, curses followed them. That which God had intended to be a blessing became a curse to His people. Their behavior did not match what was agreed in the covenants and so the covenants failed. God found fault with these covenants, His purpose was not to curse but to bless His people. He promised another type of covenant to His people. David is one of the few people who enjoyed a covenant with God which pictured the New Testament, a covenant which ensured one of his descendants will be on the throne unconditionally.

### Another

*"For if that first covenant had been faultless, then no place would have been sought for a second. Because finding fault with them, He says: "Behold, the days are coming, says the LORD, when I will make a new covenant with the house of Israel and with the house of Judah— "not according to the covenant that I made with their fathers in the day when I took them by the hand to lead them out of the land of Egypt; because they did not continue in My covenant, and I disregarded them, says the LORD. "For this is the covenant that I will make with the house of Israel after those days, says the LORD: I will put my laws in their mind and write them on their hearts; and I will be their God, and they shall be my people. "None of them shall teach his neighbor, and none his*

*brother, saying, 'Know the LORD,' for all shall know me, from the least of them to the greatest of them. "For I will be merciful to their unrighteousness, and their sins and their lawless deeds I will remember no more." In that He says, "A new covenant," He has made the first obsolete. Now what is becoming obsolete and growing old is ready to vanish away."* ( Heb 8:7-13, Jer 31:31-34)

At a point when Israel and Judah had violated the covenant and on the verge of Judah's captivity to Babylon, God makes a promise of another covenant which He promises to be completely different from the former covenants which were conditional and depended on men to keep their part to sustain it. In this one, His intention is to bless man without man having to play apart. Sin was the basis of failure of those covenants and He declared He will be merciful to their unrighteousness and their sins He will not remember, thus closing every loophole for failure.

In the New Testament, the word covenant comes with completely different meaning. Its common knowledge that the New Testament was written in Greek and not Hebrew as the Old Testament. The Greek word used in the New Testament for covenants is (diayhkh diatheke*)* "*diatheke*" and it means 'the last disposition which one makes concerning his possession after his death, a testament or a will.' Its completely different from an agreement which two parties enter into with each partner having a part to play to sustain the treaty.

In this testament God consulted no one, He entered into an agreement with none but cut out a testament for us Himself. (Heb

6:18-19), Just as He swore to Abraham by Himself by two unchangeable things in which it is impossible for God to lie, two unchangeable things, God and God. He entered into a covenant with Himself. He became the mediator and the guarantor of this testament. This testament is not guaranteed on your faithfulness, it is guaranteed by His faithfulness, even if we become unfaithful it will still stand because God cannot deny Himself, He remains faithful, (2 Tim 2:13).

*"so much the more also is the Covenant of which Jesus has become the guarantor, a better covenant. "* ( Heb 7:22, RSV)

*"And for this reason He is the Mediator of the new covenant, by means of death, for the redemption of the transgressions under the first covenant, that those who are called may receive the promise of the eternal inheritance. "* ( Heb 9:15, NKJV)

Often when we go to banks to ask for loans, the banks will ask for a guarantor or collateral. In case you fail to pay the loan the guarantor will be responsible for paying it for you. Christ became the guarantor of this testament so that it will not be dependent on our behavior as the first one was.

**The New Testament is not about an agreement of two parties but it's about a will written for us, about inheritance**. Where a will is involved the death of the testator must be established, Christ had to die to enforce the will. As long as the writer of the will still lives there is a possibility of changing the will but He died and sealed it with His own blood, now He lives by the Holy

Spirit our attorney revealing it to us. Listen to this, in Ber-eeth the covenant ceases when one of the partner dies but in diatheke the will comes into force when the writer of the will dies. *"For where there is a testament, there must also of necessity be the death of the testator. For a testament is in force after men are dead, since it has no power at all while the testator lives."* (Heb 9:16-17).

The New Testament is about what God has done for mankind and it's upon man to discover what has been done for him and walk in it. **The language of the old is do, do, do, the language of the new is DONE.** It's not about us keeping our part of the bargain, one man did it all and has become the guarantor of it, it is not guaranteed on your behavior otherwise it will fail like the former. We have majored in preaching about behavior modification in our churches as if this testament was based on behavior, no, if it was, it will automatically fail. It's not about keeping rules and laws but the discovery of the finished work of Christ on the cross and enjoying the fruit of it, God has done enough through the cross that when we discover we shall not struggle with behavior, we will find a new life which is led of the Spirit of God flowing through us, we shall enjoy God's own life. God understood clearly the weakness of man under the first covenant and He could not repeat the same thing again otherwise the results could have been the same.

*Previously saying, "Sacrifice and offering, burnt offerings, and offerings for sin you did not desire, nor had pleasure in them" (which are offered according to the law), then He said, "Behold, I have come to do Your will, O God." He takes away the first that He may establish the second.* "(Heb 10:8-9). The first is obsolete, has grown old and is vanishing away, but we still preach it as if it is the one in use. We should understand that the covenant changed and God intends for His people to walk in the new not in the old. We need to rightfully divide the word. We study the old to discover the new. The New Testament was hidden in the old.

God has cut a will for us and it's our duty to walk in it. That's why sonship has been introduced in this testament. It's sons who inherit. We are no longer in the days of ber-eeth but in the days of diatheke. It's about discovery of what has been written against your name and you take it. This is only possible through knowledge, you can not access what you don't know and the church has to be on the fore front highlighting these realities. The Bible speaks of God's people perishing for lack of knowledge (Hosea 4:6), this should be our understanding resulting in possessing what belongs to us, otherwise religion will continue making a mockery of us even after the cross. Could we for once ask ourselves what we have gained from the cross? Why live our lives as the people of the old who lived in another covenant? There is a better covenant with better promises. It does not have promises of curses. May the Holy Spirit help you discover what we have freely received in Christ.

*"As His divine power has given to us all things that pertain to life and godliness, through the knowledge of Him who called us by glory and virtue,"* (2 Pet1:3). All has been given through knowledge.

God has not changed and never changes but the document and terms of administration have changed. In August 27th 2010, a new constitution was promulgated in our nation. After the promulgation the former constitution ceased to operate. We had the same president, the same prime minister, the same police force and the same courts, but their operations had completely changed under the new constitution. The police officer who could arrest you without any warrant of arrest and could abuse you could not do the same under the new document. The judges who could detain you without bail for a petty offence could no longer do the same. If a human constitution could have such an effect much more a divine document.

## The New Way

There are obvious changes which have come through the New Testament, let's consider few of these.

I.  In the Old Testament it was the jurisdiction of men to offer sacrifices to God and beg Him to receive them. Men could do all in their ability to offer the most acceptable sacrifices to God.

**In the New Testament it is God who has offered a sacrifice and is asking man to receive it.** He has offered His Son Jesus Christ on the cross and is asking man to believe in Him as the sacrificial lamb who takes away our sins and gives us eternal life. The game has changed. Christianity is not about man with his best lamb trying to persuade a God who is in a bad mood but it's about a loving God reaching out to men.

2. In the Old Testament under the law only the high priest had the privilege to access the shekinah glory of God in the Holy of Holies once in a year on the day of atonement. He entered the Holy of Holies in Jerusalem with blood for himself and blood for the entire nation. They tied a rope to his feet incase he makes a mistake and dies, no one had to go in there to get him out, but they could easily pull his body out. Getting inside the Holy of Holies meant death to anyone else.

In this testament the curtain dividing the Holy place from the Holy of Holies was torn in the middle when Christ died on the cross. It meant man could now have access to the Holy of Holies and God come out to meet man. **The distance that existed between man and God has completely been cancelled. No more distance.** God does not live any more in the Holy of Holies in Jerusalem but He lives in the hearts of people. God has become Emmanuel to His creation. We celebrate the incarnation, the Word has become flesh in us. Religion thrives on preaching distance between man and God. As long as God is still far away we shall need mediators to stand in the gap and tell us what God says; a man of God who we have to depend on to access God's blessings on our behalf. This is so crucial for religion to thrive. We have one mediator the man Christ Jesus.

Saul on his way to Damascus, not to win souls for the kingdom but to arrest and kill those who believed in Christ, had a rear encounter with Christ. Christ appears to him. He never sent an angel, but appeared Himself to this murderer, not to kill him but to change his life. God can appear to any person any where regardless of his position in society. A Muslim sheikh conducting Islamic prayers in a mosque came out of the mosque one day confessing Christ Jesus had appeared to him and he became a believer. God has reconciled His creation to Himself, no more distance. There are numerous testimonies of people whom society had given up on. They were considered the worst of sinners, but today those same individuals are worshiping God with sincerity of heart. God took the initiative to reach them. God never came to our lives to visit but to stay. Anytime I travel for missions I carry only a small luggage of basic essentials, because I'm visiting shortly, when God came into your life, He never came to visit but to stay. He came with everything He owns and Has made your life suitable for His habitation and His comfort.

We no longer go in and come out as David sung, He abides in us 24/7. Sometime we pray "Father I come to you in the name of Jesus," where have you been that you have to come? You live in His presence daily. We often ask Him to come and join us in our meetings, We are 2000 years late. It is He who promised never to leave us nor forsake us and wherever two or three are gathered in His name He is there. We have to realign our thinking to what has happened. Many songs we sing today in our Christian worship have lost relevance. We should tune our worship to the reality of the time.

3.  In the Old Testament, all the men of God we know were either friends of God or servants of God or men after God's own heart, none were referred to as the sons of God. Jesus says, *"among all born of women (before the cross) there was none like John the Baptist but whoever is least in this kingdom is greater than John."* (Matt 11:11)

    In this testament sonship has been introduced, Whoever is least in this kingdom is greater than John. Servants have no right to inheritance but sons have the right to inherit, (1Jn 3:2). We have been born from above. As He is so are we in this world. God can not see us outside of Christ.

4.  In the old covenant, the laws were introduced to reveal how sinful man had become, *"sin indeed was in the world before the law was given, but sin is not counted where there is no law."* (Rom 5:13), also (Rom 4:15, RSV).

    *"Law came in, to increase the trespass; but where sin increased, grace abounded all the more,"* (Rom 5:20, RSV)

    In this testament, grace has come to reveal how righteous we have become in Christ Jesus. *"so that, as sin reigned in death, grace also might reign through righteousness to eternal life through Jesus Christ our Lord."* (Rom 5:21, RSV)

Grace reigns through our understanding of how righteous we have become in Christ Jesus our Lord. The law was given through Moses but grace and truth came through Jesus Christ, grace is a person, it is Christ Himself. (Rom1:17). In the Gospel the righteousness from God is revealed. Man has been justified but does not know it until the gospel reveals it. *"who was delivered up because of our offences, and was raised up because of our being declared righteous."* ((Rom 4:25, YLT). Had Christ not satisfied the judgment over our sins the grave could have laid a claim on Him.

5.  The High priest entered the Holy of Holies and stood before the mercy seat, not the throne of grace. In general understanding mercy and grace don't mean the same. A man once stole his neighbor's goat, he was arrested and taken before a court of law. He was found guilty and before the judge delivered his sentence he asked the man to plead. The man admitted to committing the crime and said he was the sole provider for his family and should he be jailed they will seriously suffer.

    The judge declared "this court finds you guilty of the crime of stealing a goat belonging to your neighbor and the sentence this court should give you is two years in jail but because of your plea, this court has had mercy on you and charged you a fine of $1,000 or failure to pay this you will be jailed for six months." This is mercy. Grace declares the man guilty, sets him free without any fine and offers him the opportunity to seat with the judge at his throne. Mercy means we don't get what we deserve, grace means we get what we never deserved. Those saints of the old enjoyed God's mercy on credit, it had not been paid for. Today it has fully been paid for at the cross and God has poured grace on us.

We are seated with Christ in heavenly places. We don't stand before the mercy seat. We have access to the throne of grace. **We are no longer praying towards the throne room, but from the throne room**. We have wasted so much time trying to get "there" when "there" is where we are! We are co-seated together with Christ because of God's doing! While we were still dead in our sins God co-quickened us and co-raised us and co-elevated us to be joint seated together with him! (Eph 2:6)

These are just a few of the many changes that took place in this testament. With this understanding of what took place in Christ and the knowledge of a changed covenant, we should no longer be subject to the old covenant but be partakers in the new dispensation and change our thinking patterns to align ourselves with the reality at hand. But the most unfortunate thing is our continual involvement with the past as if our destiny still depends on it. Many of our preaching and teachings are still based on the old dispensation which is not wrong as long as we understand how to divide the scriptures and stop preaching conditional blessings and curses.

We threaten God's people with curses wherever we feel they should do something for the kingdom of God. That belongs to the past. The ground has moved and we should tell them Christ became a curse for us so that no curses today can be preached in our churches and none should affect their lives. As long as we continue walking in this blindness of the past we empower the enemy, we join hands with the enemy to frustrate the finished work of Christ.

The Old Testament is a shadow not the reality and it's easy to manipulate people using shadows because it has no light and can't be seen clearly. The light has come. Let us walk in the light and darkness will not rule over us. We study the old to discover the new. There are many pictures of the new hidden in the old. The new is now here, lets enjoy it. The next chapter will expound on this in details.

# *THREE*

## THE LAW

*"And this is eternal life, that they may know You, the only true God, and Jesus Christ whom You have sent."* (John 17:3)

What a joy that eternity has become our destiny, God is neither ashamed nor apologetic to invite us to share in His life, the life He lives. This life does not begin in heaven but begins here on earth. Eternal life is not subject to keeping rules and statutes but the expression of the inner life we have become. Fruits are effortless spontaneous manifestation of the character of a tree. It effortlessly brings forth fruit after its own kind. And we too like trees effortlessly are supposed to manifest the fruit of the Spirit who lives in us. *Love, joy, peace, longsuffering, goodness, gentleness, faith, meekness and temperance. Against such there is no law,* (Gal 5:22-23).

This is what God expects of us, we carry His seed and there is no law which God keeps but the results are obvious. Life is not about keeping rules and regulations as many of us today have reduced Christianity to. The moment we turn Christianity to observation of rules and laws we make it no different from other human religions. Our Father wants us to enjoy His divine life which effortlessly manifests through us. As He is, so are we in this world.

What purpose then serves the law? The scripture is very clear, *"Why, then, was the law given? It was given alongside the promise to show people their sins. But the law was designed to last only until the coming of the child who was promised. God gave his law through angels to Moses, who was the mediator between God and the people. Now a mediator is helpful if more than one party must reach an agreement. But God, who is one, did not use a mediator when he gave his promise to Abraham. Is there a conflict, then, between God's law and God's promises? Absolutely not! If the law could give us new life, we could be made right with God by obeying it. But the Scriptures declare that we are all prisoners of sin, so we receive God's promise of freedom only by believing in Jesus Christ. Before the way of faith in Christ was available to us, we were placed under guard by the law. We were kept in protective custody, so to speak, until the way of faith was revealed. Let me put it another way. The law was our guardian until Christ came; it protected us until we could be made right with God through faith. And now that the way of faith has come, we no longer need the law as our guardian. For you are all children of God through faith in Christ Jesus."* (Galatians 3:19-26, NLT)

The law of Moses was given much later after the promise of God to Abraham. It came as our guardian until we could be made right with God through faith. The law was only to last till the Child Jesus Christ comes. Now that Christ has come, we cannot hold onto the law. It's like a mother holding on to the placenta after giving birth. **You can't hold on to the placenta and forsake the**

**child or hold onto both the child and the placenta.** We should stick only with the child of promise. The law was added because of transgressions till the seed of promise comes.

Since the fall of Adam sin entered the world, but man could not know sin without a law that showed him what was wrong. *"For until the law sin was in the world, **but sin is not imputed when there is no law.**"* (Rom 5:13). *"because the law brings about wrath; **for where there is no law there is no transgression,**"* (Rom 4:15). God gave the law to the Jews not to make the people righteous but to reveal how sinful man had become, to know sin. It revealed the weakness in man to live righteously and sin which had taken man captive.

It was never given to help them go to heaven or manifest the life of God, but to do the opposite, to be broken so that man can not have hope of attaining righteousness by his own efforts and to turn to God to be justified by faith. It was to disqualify man. The scriptures we've read show us that where there is no law there is no sin. Imagine driving in a highway without any traffic rules, you can make a U turn any where, you can drive in any lane, you can keep left or right and no officer will arrest you. That's how life was before the law was introduced. There was nothing you could be held accountable for lack of knowledge though sin was present. The law came in so that we can discover it is wrong to drive on the wrong side of the road, to make a stop in the middle of a highway, to make us know what is wrong and awaken sin consciousness in our lives.

*"What shall we say then? Is the law sin? Certainly not! On the contrary,* **I would not have known sin except through the law.** *For I would not have known covetousness unless the law had said, "You shall not covet." But sin, taking opportunity by the commandment, produced in me all manner of evil desire. For apart from the law sin was dead. I was alive once without the law, but* **when the commandment came, sin revived** *and I died."* (Rom 7:7-9)

*"Moreover the law entered that the* **offense might abound.** *But where sin abounded, grace abounded much more,"* (Rom 5:20)

*"Therefore by the deeds of the law no flesh will be justified in His sight, for* **by the law is the knowledge of sin.** *"* (Rom 3:20)

*"The sting of death is sin,* **and the power of sin is the law.** *"* (1 Cor 15:56, NLT)

***"For as many as are of the works of the law are under the curse;*** *for it is written, "Cursed is everyone who does not continue in all things which are written in the book of the law, to do them."* (Gal 3:10).

It's unfortunate how the devil has succeeded in blindfolding many people today who are still held captive in observing the laws of Moses thinking they will please God or earn the favor of God. The law's purpose was to do the opposite, to make us sinners, empower sin, revive sin, reveal sin, bring curses and bring wrath. Religion has reduced many of us to be observers in our Christian walk. We only admire the life of God from the scriptures but fail to enjoy it because religion has put a stumbling block of the laws of Moses on our way.

The law brings the knowledge of sin not the knowledge of righteousness. Its purpose was to make sin abound and manifest. Whoever employs the law in their life should expect sin to abound and manifest. Paul discovers in Rom 7 he could not meet the demands of the law. Covetousness which was forbidden by the Ten Commandments became his biggest obstacle in life. He tried to avoid coveting but the more he tried the more he fell into the trap of covetousness. The law enforces a do it yourself attitude. It is a system which promotes human effort to achieve the righteousness of God. To become like God by human effort. The devil tried it in heaven to be like God by his own efforts but he failed and introduced it to Adam to be like God by his own effort of eating the forbidden fruit. Adam was already like God, and now he has introduced it to us to try attaining God's life by our own effort. This was a system which Adam deliberately subjected himself to. It was in operation even before the law was given since death was also in operation. God brought it to the surface through the commandments that man may know the system at work. A system of trying to be like God without God.

The power of sin is the law. Sin took opportunity offered by the commandment to manifest and rule our lives. Covetousness was energized in Paul's life by the law. I came home with a wrapped little box one time. It was a gift for my boy's birthday. Since the day of the event hadn't come yet, I kept the box somewhere in the house. My son saw it but was not very curious to know much about its content. Then one day I told him, "boy, don't open that box." He asked "what is inside?" I told him "don't open it, period." He become more curious about knowing its content. He was not curious before but now after I had given a warning he looked for an opportunity to unwrap the box and know the content. That's what the law does. The law is holy in the sense that it points out sin, but unfortunately it does not empower us to conquer sin but empowers sin in our lives. When you awaken sin consciousness in your life, the result is you will walk in sin. God doesn't intend for us to walk with a sin consciousness but a son consciousness.. So to remove sin and curses, the law had to go.

We cannot enjoy the life God intended for us by observing the law. The law will make you conscious of sin. **The knowledge and consciousness of sin will empower you to walk in sin and the knowledge and consciousness of righteousness will empower you to walk in righteousness.** Any believer who knows he is a sinner as the law states and tries to be righteous, will often struggle to live a righteous life. But whoever has the awareness of being righteous will automatically manifest what he believes he is. You discover you are righteous and the consequences of righteousness manifests. *"For as he thinks in his heart, so is he."* (Pro 23:7). The latter kills but the Spirit gives life. From its inception the law had begun doing its purpose, to kill. *"so the sons of Levi did according to the word of Moses. And about three thousand men of the people fell that day."* (Exodus 32:28). Let's consider some few issues which come up when the law was given and when the Spirit of Life came on the day of Pentecost.

| | |
|---|---|
| 1) Exo 32:28. When Moses come with the Ten Commandments 3000 men died. | Acts 2:41 On the day of Pentecost in Jerusalem, 3000 men believed. |
| 2 Exo 19:18, The mountain was wrapped up in fire and smoke. | Acts 2:3. Cloven tongues of fire appeared on the disciples. The connection was now closer, God was nolonger far from His people, He had connected Himself to them. |
| 3 Exo. 20:1 God spoke from the mountain to the Jews. Jewish historians believe God spoke in multiple languages when he gave the law. | Acts 2:4. They spoke in varieties of tongues as the Spirit gave them utterance. God spoke through them not from the mountain. The connection was intimate. |
| 4 Exo. 19:23. The Jews were warned not to come up the mountain, nor touch the mountain but to remain at the foot of the mountain. The law drives us away from God. | Acts 1:13. The disciples were looked up in an upper room, not at the foot of a mountain. The Spirit brings us to God. |
| 5 Exo. 34:29-35. When Moses come from the mountain, his face shone and the people could not come near Him. The law looks glorious but drives us from God. | Acts 2:6. The multitudes in Jerusalem run to the disciples when they heard them speak in tongues. The anointing of God attracts people. |

## Law and Faith

*"Yet the law is not of faith,* but *"the man who does them shall live by them."* (Gal 3:12). Those who live by the law can not please God (Hebrews 11:6). Law has nothing to do with faith. You can not live by the Ten Commandments and claim to have faith in God, no it can't work that way. Whoever practices the law has distanced himself from the life of faith, he has credited his success and achievements by his obedience to the law, by his best efforts and best performance and that is not of faith. *"To him who works the wages are not counted as grace but as debt."* (Rom 4:4)

The Purpose of the law was to reveal our sinfulness, it drove men far from God. I heard Joseph prince giving this illustration from the scripture regarding Moses the law giver who could not fulfill the demands of the law. In (Hebrews 11), Moses is mentioned among the men of God who accomplished great things by faith.

*"By faith Moses, when he was born, was hidden three months by his parents, because they saw he was a beautiful child; and they were not afraid of the king's command. By faith Moses, when he became of age, refused to be called the son of Pharaoh's daughter, choosing rather to suffer affliction with the people of God than to enjoy the passing pleasures of sin, esteeming the reproach of Christ greater riches than the treasures in Egypt; for he looked to the reward. By faith he forsook Egypt, not fearing the wrath of the king; for he endured as seeing Him who is invisible. By faith he kept the Passover and the sprinkling of blood, lest he who destroyed the firstborn should touch them. By faith they passed through the Red Sea as by dry land, whereas the Egyptians, attempting to do so, were drowned."* (Hebrews 11:23-29).

All the great achievements of Moses were before the law was given, after the law was given at Mount Sinai, Moses accomplished nothing of faith. With the law there is no faith, the law does not recognize faith but self effort.

See also this example in the Gospels, Jesus acknowledged the unique faith of two individuals, the Roman centurion (Mathew 8:5-13), and the Canaanite woman (Mathew 15:21-28). These two individuals had one thing in common, they were all gentiles, they knew nothing about the law of Moses and they could easily believe Jesus for the supernatural. Whenever we subject ourselves under the teaching of the law we forfeit faith, you can not mix faith with the law, the law reveals your weakness and requires your own effort which is contrary to faith which requires you to believe on God's work and not on your work. We kill peoples' faith in God by subjecting them under the teachings of the law, (Rom 4:4-5).

### The LAW Brings Wrath

The children of Israel left Egypt under Abrahamic covenant. God had promised Abraham He will deliver his descendants from captivity with a heavy hand and take them to the land of promise. (Gen 15:13-20). God delivered them from Egypt with a mighty hand and protected them from their enemies. *"Now when they came to Marah, they could not drink the waters of Marah, for they were bitter. Therefore the name of it was called Marah. And the people complained against Moses, saying, "What shall we drink?"* (Exodus 15:23-24)

The people complained but God did not punish them for complaining. *"Then the whole congregation of the children of Israel complained against Moses and Aaron in the wilderness. And the children of Israel said to them, "Oh, that we had died by the hand of the LORD in the land of Egypt, when we sat by the pots of meat and when we ate bread to the full! For you have brought us out into this wilderness to kill this whole assembly with hunger."* (Exodus 16:2-3). They complained again against Moses and God but none of them was punished.

*"Then all the congregation of the children of Israel set out on their journey from the Wilderness of Sin, according to the*

*commandment of the LORD, and camped in Rephidim; but there was no water for the people to drink. Therefore the people contended with Moses, and said, "Give us water, that we may drink." And Moses said to them, "Why do you contend with me? Why do you tempt the LORD?" And the people thirsted there for water, and the people complained against Moses, and said, "Why is it you have brought us up out of Egypt, to kill us and our children and our livestock with thirst?" So Moses cried out to the LORD, saying, "What shall I do with this people? They are almost ready to stone me."* (Exodus 17:1-4). None of them was punished for complaining and murmuring.

Immediately after the law was given, any time they complained against Moses or God they were punished and thousands died. *"But while the meat was still between their teeth, before it was chewed, the wrath of the LORD was aroused against the people, and the LORD struck the people with a very great plague. So he called the name of that place Kibroth Hattaavah, because there they buried the people who had yielded to craving."* (Numbers 11:33-34). Also in (Num 12, 14,16,21,25). Paul warns us of following after their example, *"But with many of them God was not well pleased: for they were overthrown in the wilderness. Now these things were our examples, to the intent we should not lust after evil things, as they also lusted. Neither be ye idolaters, as were some of them; as it is written, the people sat down to eat and drink, and rose up to play. Neither let us commit fornication, as some of them committed, and fell in one day three and twenty thousand. Neither let us tempt Christ, as some of them also tempted and were destroyed of serpents. Neither murmur ye, as some of them also murmured, and were destroyed of the destroyer. Now all these things happened unto them for ensembles: and they are written for our admonition, upon whom the ends of the world are come"* (1 Cor 10:5-11).

The law attracts wrath not favor, any moment we walk under the law we attract wrath and that's its purpose, (Rom 4:15). Many of our preaching are full of wrath, we threaten people with God's wrath if they don't fulfill some demands of the law, this is legalism at its best which God hates. We set rules for prayers, for fasting, for giving, for reading the Bible, for attending church. There is a difference between discipline and legalism, legalism leaves you with guilt when you fail to do something. Any moment you believe God will not bless you because you never fasted or prayed or tithed then you are under the influence of legalism. No wander many Christians are struggling with a negative picture about God, they see Him as an old man holding a rod in His hands ready to strike us any moment we break the law. They have made God in their own image. **Hostility separates people more than distance or time.** Remember the covenant has changed and in this testament God does not remember our sins.

How does He punish us if He can't remember our sins? It pleases the enemy to keep us under the law not to experience the love and favor of God. Before the law was given, there was sin but sin was not accounted for, but after the law was given they faced the consequences of their misbehavior according to the law, they were now aware. The law must have a government or authority for it to be legal, it was ordained by angels through a mediator Moses, anytime they violated the law, the authority behind the system (angels) ensured there was punishment (Gal 3:19). A law without enforcement is not valid, it's a system which ensures punishment for violation. Whoever subjects himself under this system should not expect mercy but punishment, judgement. We are not under the system of the law, we are married to another husband, Jesus Christ, therefore we should not bring back that which is obsolete, which is fading away. We have been saved from His wrath because of Christ, (Rom 5:9).

**Additional Laws.**
It should be noted that God intended a simple covenant with Israel but because of their failure to relate with God things got complicated and it became so difficult for them to enjoy God's blessings. In (Exodus 19:1-16a), God makes a covenant with Israel just like He made with Abraham their fore father. They were to obey God (Exo. 19:5-, Gen 26:5), keep the covenant (Exo. 19:5- Gen17:1-4) and exercise faith (Exo. 19:9, Gen 15:6). They were to be a kingdom of priests and a holy nation (Exo. 19:5). They quickly agreed (Exo. 19:8) but were unable to keep the agreement.

God had intended a simple covenant with Israel not a complication of laws to obey *"For I did not speak to your fathers, or command them in the day that I brought them out of the land of Egypt, concerning burnt offerings or sacrifices. But this is what I commanded them, saying, 'Obey My voice, and I will be your*

*God, and you shall be My people. And walk in all the ways that I have commanded you that it may be well with you."* (Jer 7:22-23)

In (Exo. 19:16b-25) because of their fear of doing what God had intended for them, (Exo. 20:18-21), they were no longer a kingdom of priests but a kingdom with a priest (19:22-24). Instead of people coming up the mountain, they were refrained. Only Moses and Aaron went up (19:12-13,21-23). Instead of simple faith and obedience the decalogue (Ten Commandments) and additional laws (Covenant Code, Exo 20:22-23:33), became the basis of Israel's keeping their covenant with God. Because of their fear and failure to obey, priesthood and a tabernacle was introduced (Exo 25-31).

Ezekiel clearly states it was not God's intention to give those laws, He knew they were not good. *"And I said to their children in the wilderness, Do not walk in the statutes of your fathers, nor observe their ordinances, nor defile yourselves with their idols. I the LORD am your God; walk in my statutes, and be careful to observe my ordinances, and hallow my Sabbaths that they may be a sign between me and you, that you may know that I the LORD am your God. But the children rebelled against me; they did not walk in my statutes..........25 **Moreover I gave them statutes that were not good and ordinances by which they could not have life;"** (Eze 20:18-26, RSV). God Himself declares these laws are not good, who are we to keep teaching them and practicing them? We can not have life through the observance of the law.

(Exodus 31-). When the people fell into idolatry and worshiped the golden calf, God renewed the covenant (Exo 33-34). This resulted in the introduction of further laws to keep the priests from being involved in idolatry (Exo 35-Lev16, priestly code). (Lev17:1-9) The people again fell into idolatry by having goat idols, this saw the introduction of another set of laws (Holiness Code, Lev17-26) and a renewal of the covenant (Lev 26). It was completely impossible to satisfy the demands of the law. Anytime they broke the laws additional laws come into existence and a renewal of the covenant. God's intention was not for Israel to have life through the laws but to discover their inadequacy to keep those rules. More and more rules were added to make it even harder for them to fulfill, and none ever succeeded in fulfilling the demands of the law including Moses the law giver.

Gen 26:5 *"because Abraham obeyed My voice and kept My charge, My commandments, My statutes, and My laws."* It portrays Abraham as one who kept the Law and yet we know Abraham lived before the introduction of the law, he obeyed God by faith and it was accounted to him as righteousness. *"Then the LORD spoke to Moses and Aaron, "Because you did not believe Me, to hallow Me in the eyes of the children of Israel, therefore you shall not bring this assembly into the land which I have given them."* (Num 20:12). It portrays Moses the giver of the law as one who did not believe. It is not the keeping of the law that justifies us but the obedience of faith which God had intended from the beginning.

## The Ten Commandments

Many times when I visit homes and offices of believers, I always get surprised to see the Ten Commandments hanged on the walls well framed. Surprisingly Paul calls them a ministry of death and condemnation. *"But if the ministry of death, written and engraved on stones, was glorious, so that the children of Israel could not look steadily at the face of Moses because of the glory of his countenance, which glory was passing away, how will the ministry of the Spirit not be more glorious? For if the ministry of condemnation had glory, the ministry of righteousness exceeds much more in glory."* (2 Cor 3:7-9).

We know of all the commandments given to Moses. It's the Ten Commandments that were engraved in stones. He calls them a ministry of death, it brings memory of sin in our lives, it awakens sin consciousness in our lives. Paul says in Romans 7 how he was alive until the commandment came, when the commandment came he died. He mentions covetousness which is one of the ten. The law empowers sin in our lives and sin brings death to our lives. He calls them a ministry of condemnation. It condemns us, it shows us our inadequacy to live as God intended for us and makes alive the urge to sin. It always demands righteousness from us and when we fail it condemns us. **The law will always demand but will not lift a finger to help you achieve its demands but grace supplies righteousness without us lifting a finger.** The law always points to us, you shall...., you shall...., but grace points us to what Christ has done not about us but about Him. In Vs 10, Paul calls it *"what is passing away was glorious,* *what remains is much more glorious."* This thing has passed away, it will be better if you take those commandments to the house of unbeliever, he may try to live by them and fail and will be convicted to turn to God's grace for salvation.

*"But we know that the law is good if one uses it lawfully, knowing this: **that the law is not made for a righteous person, but for the lawless** and insubordinate, for the ungodly and for sinners, for the unholy and profane, for murderers of fathers and murderers of mothers, for manslayers, for fornicators, for sodomites, for kidnappers, for liars, for perjurers, and if there is any other thing that is contrary to sound doctrine, according to the glorious gospel of the blessed God which was committed to my trust."* (1 Tim 1:8-11).

The law is not for us who have become the righteousness of God by faith. Its for unbelievers who need to know they lack the power to keep the law and turn to God's grace for salvation. Is it not surprising that in most Christian meetings we subject believers again to commandments and we think they are the most holy things we need to teach our people? When we do this we are killing people, not giving them life. This is a ministry which brings death to your life, it suffocates you of faith in God, it awakens your mind to sin and wherever you fail to keep them it leaves you with condemnation. The law is the tree of the knowledge of good and evil. When you eat it you discover your nakedness, you see how sinful you are. It puts an urge in you to try to cover yourself by your works or efforts.

This is the weapon the devil has used all along to condemn us. Christ disarmed the devil by fulfilling the law and taking it away from our lives as a demand we should keep. It is not God's plan for a believer to walk in condemnation, Paul after his struggle with the commandments in (Rom 7: 24- 25), he writes what a wretched man he was, who will save him from this body of death. He finds the answer and writes, 'thanks to God through Jesus Christ.' He begins chapter eight by saying *"therefore there is no condemnation to everyone who is in Christ Jesus."* The original writings do not have the phrase *"who walk in the spirit and not in the flesh,"* that is an addition from the translators who could not figure out how someone could live without condemnation from God and they added their own conditions. When should one be condemned, when he sins or when he has not sinned? Obvious it is when he sins, but God says there is no condemnation even when we sin. Why? Because Christ was condemned on my behalf for my sins that's why God will never condemn me again. You can't punish one offence twice. There is no condemnation to us in Christ, the law promotes condemnation. God intends you to live in joy and peace. When you feel your heart condemns you remember God is greater than your heart, run to what God says.

### Jesus and the Law.

Jesus was raised as a Jew born under the law to redeem those under the law (Gal 4:4-5). He understood the very purposes of the law. Many people in the religious circles still believe Jesus did not come to remove the law but to strengthen the law. *"Do not think that I came to destroy the Law or the Prophets. I did not come to destroy but to fulfill. "For assuredly, I say to you, till heaven and earth pass away, one jot or one title will by no means pass from the law till all is fulfilled. "* (Matt 5:17).

Jesus after teaching about the heavenly attitudes in Mathew 5 which were completely strange to the law of Moses, He affirms His mission as far as the law is concerned. To preach to a Jewish congregation He had to make His position known. He did not come to destroy the law but to fulfill it. The law spoke of Christ in its ordinances and He came to fulfill what the law had pictured for many years. No single dot of God's word can be done away with without being fulfilled. Christ fulfilled the law. *"Then He said to them, "These are the words which I spoke to you while I was still with you, that all things must be fulfilled which were written in the Law of Moses and the Prophets and the Psalms concerning Me." And He opened their understanding, that they might comprehend the Scriptures. "* (Luke 24:44-45).

**He fulfilled the law by becoming sin and dyeing to sin according to the demands of the law**. *"The wages of sin is death, "* (Rom 6:23), one died for sin fulfilling the demand of the law. He became the sacrifice for sin pictured by the law. He was the only individual since the law was given through Moses who attained the righteous requirements of the law. The Jews had a standard which they were familiar with as far as keeping the law was concerned, Some Pharisees like Paul could boast of being blameless in keeping the law (Phil 3:6). Christ comes and raises the bar even much higher to those who thought they could fulfill the law. Under the law, the Pharisees seemed to have attained righteousness, but Christ declares they have not, He demands we go beyond the righteousness of the Pharisees. *"Unless your righteousness exceeds the Pharisees you will not enter the kingdom of heaven"* (Matt 5:20). The righteousness by faith in Christ far exceeds the Pharisees self righteousness by works.

Committing adultery was sin according to the law, Jesus declares looking at a woman lustfully is already committing adultery. Killing someone was breaking the law, Jesus declares hating someone was equal to killing. If one asks you take them one mile, Jesus says you double that, if he takes your tunic you give him your coat also. The law demanded an eye for an eye but Jesus declares if one slaps you on the right you turn to them the left chick also. If your eyes causes you to sin gauge it out, the likes of Paul who struggled with covetousness could have gauged off their eyes. He makes it much difficult for those who thought they could fulfill the demands of the law. If your hands makes you to sin cut it off, be perfect by human effort as God is perfect. The failure to keep these standards was hell (Matt 5:29, 45). Christ was discouraging them from seeking justification through the law, He was showing them it is impossible to meet God's standards of righteousness by the law i.e, do it yourself, otherwise the nation could be full of blind folks without limbs. The young rich ruler left sad and the Pharisees left mad.

The law knew nothing about mercy, peace making, purity of heart, meekness, poor in spirit, but even these beatitudes were a system of do it yourself, it promoted human effort. In some instances Jesus asked the people He had healed to go offer sacrifices as the law commanded, He was in a Jewish territory and the law was still in operation, a new covenant had not been initiated by His blood on Calvary. When He dealt with Pharisees He gave them the law, but when He spoke to His disciples He introduced them to grace. He declared you can't put new wine into old wineskins, they will burst. New wine, new wine skins, old wine, old wineskins (Matt 9:17). He had not yet died on the cross for sins as the law demanded, and asked those who still believed in the law to do as the law required but He never asked any gentile to go and offer the sacrifices Moses spoke of. Gentiles were never subject to the law of Moses and so we are not supposed to. The new covenant does not begin in Mathew chapter one, it begins operation after the shedding of blood at Calvary. No covenant could be established without shedding of blood.

*"For Christ is the end of the law for righteousness to everyone who believes."* (Rom 10:4) *"For all the prophets and the law prophesied until John;"* (Matt 11:13). **Christ fulfilled the law thus qualified to remove the law from the path of the righteous** and prophesied a new way to come free from rules and regulations. Grace and law cannot operate together, grace and truth came by Jesus Christ. We can not balance the two, you are either under law (self effort, performance, D.I.Y, do it yourself) or under grace (believing in what God has done).

The New Testament is the revelation of God's initiative and grace gift to mankind. While **the law system addresses man in Adam, grace reveals and addresses man in Christ**. The law demands righteousness while grace supplies righteousness. As long as you walk under the law there will always be a demand for you to be righteous and yet you won't be able to meet the demand. Under grace you will always be confident of walking in Christ's righteousness, it's a done deal. The righteous requirements of the law have been met in us not by us, (Rom 8:4).

*"Having wiped out the handwriting of requirements that was against us, which was contrary to us. And He has taken it out of the way, having nailed it to the cross."* (Col 2:14).

*"Having abolished in His flesh the enmity, that is, the law of commandments contained in ordinances, so as to create in Himself one new man from the two, thus making peace."* (Eph 2:15).

Under the law, a Jew and a gentile could not associate, He removed the law which was the cause of hostility, the law was full of requirements which were against us, and He nailed it on the cross when He was crucified. He has removed the law from being a stumbling block to us and gave us His Spirit. *"But the fruit of the Spirit is love, joy, peace, longsuffering, kindness, goodness, faithfulness, gentleness, and self-control. Against such there is no law,"* (Gal 5:22-23). This is the basis of the Christian life not laws and regulations. Whoever manifests the fruit of the Spirit in his life does not need the Ten Commandments. Love is the fulfillment of the law. Besides discouraging the Jews about living by the law, Christ also prophesied of a coming covenant where law will not be the standard for living, they will enjoy the life of God without condemnation, He pictures this in the parable of the prodigal son.

*"Therefore, my brethren, you also have become dead to the law through the body of Christ, that you may be married to another—to Him who was raised from the dead, that we should bear fruit to God......But now we have been delivered from the law, having died to what we were held by, so that we should serve in the newness of the Spirit and not in the oldness of the letter."* (Rom 7:4,6).

*"For sin shall not have dominion over you, for you are not under law but under grace."* (Rom 6:13)

We are dead to the law, we can not walk in it any more, to do so will be like denying the death of Christ on the cross where he nailed the law and set us free from its demands, we shall be choosing Moses over Jesus Christ, we shall be choosing the commandments over the fruit of the Spirit and we shall be choosing legalism over the life of faith. We had to die to the law to be married to a new husband, as long as we live by the law we can not be married to another husband who is Christ, we can not be married to two husbands at once, either choose the law or Christ.

### The Jerusalem Church
On the day of Pentecost when the church was born, Peter stood in the crowds and quotes prophet Joel (Acts 2:17-21, Joel 2:28-32). He boldly declares *"and it shall come to pass, that whosoever shall call on the name of the Lord shall be saved."* (Acts 2:21)

Whosoever basically implies anyone, whether Jew or gentile, unfortunately **it took Peter ten years to preach to a gentile.**

It took the intervention of God through a vision at Joppa to let Peter understand what God has cleansed he had no reason to call common (Acts 10:9-16). Peter like all other Jews was still bound to the Jewish traditions even after the Pentecostal experience, they were still trapped like many of us today to the Jewish customs. According to the Jewish tradition a Jew was never allowed to enter the house of a gentile or shake hands with a gentile otherwise he risked becoming unclean.

Should we allow ourselves to be under the law we should be ready to be separate from the Jews. After this experience at Joppa, Peter got the boldness to enter the house of Cornelius a Roman officer. A council was summoned to address why Peter preached to gentiles, he had a hard task to explain to the believers in Jerusalem why he entered the house of a gentile and preached to them. This was the mindset of the believers in Jerusalem.

When the council concluded its deliberations it was fully agreed that the gentiles should not be subjected to the law of Moses, (Acts:15) but how comes we try to do the opposite today? We are not Jews but gentiles, the law was not given to the gentiles but Jews, we were not part of the old covenants, we are foreigners to the covenants under the law. **I suggest we need another Jerusalem council** to remind us again that we gentiles are not part of the law of Moses.

Peter was still bound by these same traditions years later when he went to Antioch, Paul had to openly rebuke him before the conference. *"Now when Peter had come to Antioch, I withstood him to his face, because he was to be blamed; for before certain men came from James, he would eat with the Gentiles; but when they came, he withdrew and separated himself, fearing those who were of the circumcision. And the rest of the Jews also played the hypocrite with him, so that even Barnabas was carried away with their hypocrisy. But when I saw that they were not straightforward about the truth of the gospel, I said to Peter before them all, "If you, being a Jew, live in the manner of Gentiles and not as the Jews, why do you compel Gentiles to live as Jews? "We who are Jews by nature, and not sinners of the Gentiles. "* (Gal 2:11-15).

The Jerusalem church was deeply involved in Judaism. We have no reference in Acts of the believers in Jerusalem being referred to as Christians. The gentile church in Antioch were the first to be called Christians, they knew nothing of the law of Moses. Paul returns to Jerusalem after his third missionary Journey, he encounters the legalism going on in Jerusalem church. *"And when we had come to Jerusalem, the brethren received us gladly. On the following day Paul went in with us to James, and all the elders were present. When he had greeted them, he told in detail those things which God had done among the Gentiles through his ministry. And when they heard it, they glorified the Lord. And they said to him, "**You see, brother, how many myriads of Jews there are who have believed, and they are all zealous for the law;** "but they have been informed about you that you teach all the Jews who are among the Gentiles to forsake Moses, saying that they ought not to circumcise their children nor to walk* *according to the customs." What then? The assembly must certainly meet, for they will hear that you have come. "Therefore do what we tell you: We have four men who have taken a vow. "Take them and be purified with them, and pay their expenses so that they may shave their heads, and that all may know that those things of which they were informed concerning you are nothing, but that you yourself also walk orderly and keep the law."*

*"But concerning the Gentiles who believe, we have written and decided that they should observe no such thing, except that they should keep themselves from things offered to idols, from blood, from things strangled, and from sexual immorality." Then Paul took the men, and the next day, having been purified with them, entered the temple to announce the expiration of the days of purification, at which time an offering should be made for each one of them."* (Acts 21:17-26).

**Believers zealous of the law of Moses ready to kill another believer because he preached against Moses.** They were still practicing Judaism even taking vows, shaving their heads and offering according to the laws of Moses. They still believed they had to do something physically to be accepted by God, just as some of us today still believe. Paul entered into unfamiliar territory and encountered the real confusion in Jerusalem. It is not the best example for a believer today, legalism had taken root in the Jerusalem church. Historians tell us it was difficult to differentiate between Christianity and Judaism until the destruction of the Temple in A.D 70. That's when Christians continued worshiping without the temple and Judaizers were left without a place of worship. This is what we have to guard ourselves against or else we may find ourselves going the same way. Paul understood there was no other gospel apart from justification by grace and not by works. He warned the Galatians. *"if anyone preached to you another gospel let him be accursed."* (Gal 1:8-9).

## Jesus and Moses.

To the Jewish believer Moses still held a significant place in their faith, they mixed the law and grace and thought they could still obey Moses to earn justification, these are the people who caused problems wherever Paul preached to the Gentiles, they demanded the Gentiles be circumcised. Jesus took James, Peter and John to the mountain and was transfigured before them (Matt17:1-6). Moses and Elijah appeared with Jesus. Their first imagination was to put up three tents, one for Moses, another for Elijah and another for Jesus. In their understanding they had put Jesus on the same level as Moses and Elijah. God had to cancel their wrong ideology by removing Moses and Elijah from the scene and spoke from the clouds, *"this is my son in whom I am well pleased, hear him."* We cannot put Jesus on the same level with Moses and Elijah, He is the Son while they were faithful servants in the house. Peter unfortunately did not learn from this experience.

## Change of Law

According to the Levitical priesthood, all priests who served in the temple were to come from the tribe of Levi, the law did not allow anyone from a different tribe to serve as a priest. Jesus our high priest is not from the tribe of Levi but from Judah, this definitely implies the law has changed. *"Therefore, if perfection were through the Levitical priesthood (for under it the people received the law), what further need was there that another priest should rise according to the order of Melchizedek, and not be called according to the order of Aaron?* **For the priesthood being changed, of necessity there is also a change of the law.** *For He of whom these things are spoken belongs to another tribe, from which no man has officiated at the altar. For it is evident that our Lord arose from Judah, of which tribe Moses spoke nothing concerning priesthood. And it is yet far more evident if, in the likeness of Melchizedek, there arises another priest who has come, not according to the law of a fleshly commandment, but according to the power of an endless life. For He testifies: "You are a priest forever According to the order of Melchizedek. "For on the one hand there is an annulling of the former commandment because of its weakness and unprofitability, for the law made nothing perfect; on the other hand, there is the bringing in of a better hope, through which we draw near to God."* (Heb 7:11-19)

**The priesthood has changed and likewise the law has changed**, if we still operate under the former which does not recognize our high priest from the tribe of Judah, we are pouring insult to the new covenant. We should take the old with all its laws and get a priest from Levi and offer all the sacrifices the older order required, we can not take the law of the old and claim to be under the new priesthood order.

## Law Repels

*"Now a certain ruler asked Him, saying, "Good Teacher, what shall I do to inherit eternal life?" So Jesus said to him, "Why do you call me good? No one is good but One, that is, God. "You know the commandments: 'Do not commit adultery,' 'Do not murder,' 'Do not steal,' 'Do not bear false witness,' 'Honor your father and your mother.'" And he said, "All these things I have kept from my youth." So when Jesus heard these things, He said to him, "You still lack one thing. Sell all that you have and distribute to the poor, and you will have treasure in heaven; and come, follow me." But when he heard this, he became very sorrowful, for he was very rich. And when Jesus saw that he became very sorrowful, He said, "How hard it is for those who have riches to enter the kingdom of God!"For it is easier for a camel to go through the eye of a needle than for a rich man to enter the kingdom of God." And those who heard it said, "Who then can be saved?" But He said, "The things which are impossible with men are possible with God."* (Luke 18:18-27).

A certain ruler comes to Jesus, he doesn't encounter any resistance from the disciples reaching to Jesus. He was a rich respected man in society. He calls Jesus Good teacher, Jesus never denied that He was good, He affirmed that God was the only one good and accepted being put in the same level as God because He was God incarnate. The man asked "what shall I do" to enter the kingdom of God. The law demands doing, and as a faithful student of the law he approached Jesus on the basis of the law. Grace is not about doing but believing what has been done on your behalf. Jesus answers him on the basis of the law, the man brags he has done all these since he was a boy. Jesus understood the self righteousness sponsored by the law, it was based on doing things to earn God's acceptance. To be able to do things on your own, your wealth was your strength, Jesus tells him to sell all he has and follow Him, the man was extremely disappointed and left because he had put all his self righteousness on his efforts and wealth. He had failed to keep the first commandment by making his wealth his god.

Jesus asked how hard it is for rich self righteous men to enter the kingdom of God. The disciples on hearing this did not ask "how can we be saved" but they asked "who can be saved?" In their understanding a rich man was already saved because he could offer all the sacrifices the law demanded, he could do things for himself, he could attain salvation by his wealth. When this man saw he could not meet the demand of Christ, he walked away sad. Man has always tried to reach God by keeping rules but he always discovers there is a law in him that never allows him to fulfill the righteous requirements of the law. When we discover our weakness we flee away from God. **The law drives us far from God by revealing our sinfulness**, it is all about man's effort to reach God which never succeeds and leaves us feeling sinful and condemned.

*"Then Jesus entered and passed through Jericho. Now behold, there was a man named Zacchaeus who was a chief tax collector, and he was rich. And he sought to see who Jesus was, but could not because of the crowd, for he was of short stature. So he ran ahead and climbed up into a sycamore tree to see Him, for He was*

*going to pass that way. And when Jesus came to the place, He looked up and saw him, and said to him, "Zacchaeus, make haste and come down, for today I must stay at your house. "So he made haste and came down, and received Him joyfully. But when they saw it, they all complained, saying, "He has gone to be a guest with a man who is a sinner." Then Zacchaeus stood and said to the Lord, "Look, Lord, I give half of my goods to the poor; and if I have taken anything from anyone by false accusation, I restore fourfold." And Jesus said to him, "Today salvation has come to this house, because he also is a son of Abraham; "for the Son of Man has come to seek and to save that which was lost."* (Luke 19:1-10).

Jesus encounters another rich man, this man was different from the first one, he was not self righteous but he understood his position as a sinner who was unworthy even to come close to Jesus. Jesus was on his way to Jericho, Zacchaeus the tax collector got wind of Jesus passing through his town, he knew the Pharisees and religious people of his town will not allow him to come near the crowds. He was considered a sinner for working for the Roman government collecting taxes. He decided he will climb a tree just to see Jesus from a far. Jesus passes his way and asks him to come down the tree, he goes into Zacchaeus house. Zacchaeus had never hosted any religious leader in his house, they despised him and considered him a sinner. What was impossible in chapter 18 becomes possible in 19 without quoting any rules and laws, he gave his wealth to the poor and paid back all he had stolen from four times.

We were sinners not worthy of God's visitation, He come to us not on our invitation but His own initiative, not to give us rules to follow but to introduce us to Himself. When we realize what God has done on our behalf, there is no struggle in giving ourselves back to God. When Zacchaeus saw the favor Christ had bestowed on Him by coming to his house, he could not resist that love but responded to it. When we discover the grace of God in our lives we can not resist giving ourselves to God in love.

**What is impossible to achieve under the law is possible under grace**. Help your congregation to understand God's grace, it will save you much trouble in forcing them to do things. God's grace will teach them to offer their lives to God. There is no power which is stronger than love. Hate is not powerful as love, preach God's unconditional love and none can resist this. *"For I am the least of the apostles, that am not meet to be called an apostle, because I persecuted the church of God. But by the grace of God I am what I am: and his grace which was bestowed upon me was not in vain; but I labored more abundantly than they all: yet not I, but the grace of God which was with me"* (1 Cor 15:10). Paul recognized God's grace in his life, grace labored through him, the law drives us from God but grace draws us to Him. We can not continue under the law when grace is here, the life of God Himself has been poured out to us, how can we continue under a tutor when sonship and inheritance has come, when freedom is here? Jesus says *"come to me all who labor and heavy laden and I will give them rest."* (Matt 11:28) He is not addressing the so called sinners but those who have been heavily laden by the demands of the law. Let us enter His rest apart from the law. To those who are obsessed with keeping the law, why do we have to choose some section of the law and ignore others? The law was one unit, you have to keep it all or discard it all, to keep one and leave ten out you have broken it all. If anyone is passionate about the law he should keep it all and even come up with his own temple. Let's walk in this liberty Christ has set us free and enjoy the life of God.

Some people fear teaching God's grace as Paul did because they feel it renders them jobless, they think for them to be relevant to people they have to keep them busy with performance but understanding God's grace discourages self effort and performance to merit God's blessings.

Religion thrives mainly on three things, one is distance, therefore we must have someone to stand on the gap on our behalf always, second, it thrives on portraying an angry and harsh God, therefore we can not approach Him and someone has always to approach Him on our behalf, third, it thrives on guilt, the more you make people feel guilty the more dependent they will be on you. That's how the religious system works. Distance, anger and guilt. You combine the three you are left with believers who are bound and desperate. Help people believe what has been done. **The zeal for God will exhaust you, the zeal of God will ignite you.** Jesus said, *"this is the work of God that you believe on Him whom He has sent,"* (John 6:29). The work of God is believing.

# *FOUR*

## RIGHTEOUSNESS

One thing the Christian world has struggled to achieve is righteousness. It is the most talked about and most desired yet it seems to be most elusive in the perspective of the Christendom. The understanding of righteousness is key to enjoying the fruit of our redemption, it is what puts the devil where he belongs and all manner of condemnation is dealt with.

> *"For I am not ashamed of the gospel of Christ, for it is the power of God to salvation for everyone who believes, for the Jew first and also for the Greek. For in it the righteousness of God is revealed from faith to faith; as it is written, "The just shall live by faith."* (Rom 1:16-17)

Paul declares he is not ashamed of the gospel for it is the power of God to save. It's only in the Gospel of Christ that the power of God to save is revealed. All the other writings before the coming of Christ were pointing at His coming and what will happen. But the gospel reveals what has happened and the power of salvation is manifested. It's through the gospel of Christ that the power of God to save has been revealed through the cross. In it the righteousness of God is revealed from faith to faith, not the sinfulness of man being revealed but God's righteousness. We believe what God believes, we receive by faith and keep it by faith. What God has done right is revealed. **Truth is not found in the transgression,**

**in what Adam did wrong but in what God has done right in Christ**. Righteousness apart from the law has been revealed which by far surpasses the righteousness by works of the Pharisees (Matt 5:20).

As we studied earlier, no one is justified by keeping the law (Rom 3:20). Being justified through the law means Christ has become of no effect to you, you have fallen from grace, (Gal 5:3-4). Any believer who thinks he is counted righteous because he has fasted or spent hours in prayer or has won souls to the kingdom or done something for God, that believer has fallen from grace, he has made the cross of no effect in his life. When you fall in sin God's grace lifts you up again, but if you fall from grace it means you have to get everything by your own strength, you have no need of Christ. Paul says that he may be found in Him not having a righteousness that comes by the law, (Phil 3:9). As a Pharisee he pursued righteousness by fulfilling the commandments, now he discovered his own righteousness is as filthy rags. The kingdom of God is all about righteousness, Christ did not come to bring us material things on earth, man already had all the material but lacked righteousness.

He come to make us right. Jesus addressing the Jews, He told them to seek the kingdom of God, in their mind they were busy seeking an earthly king who would liberate them from the Roman rule. They already thought they were righteous by obeying the commandments. There is a righteousness that comes from above and not of the law.*"seek ye first the kingdom of God and all His righteousness and all these things shall be added to you."* (Matt 6:33).

The kingdom of God is righteousness, peace, and joy in the Holy Spirit (Rom 14:17). This is what you are supposed to enjoy.

**An Exchange.**

In God's mind, we all became sinners by one man's disobedience, Adam. We fell short of God's glory through one man's disobedience. We were all counted in Adam. Adam was the example of us and his failure was attributed to all of mankind. We became sinners not because we sinned but because Adam sinned. As it was in Adam so it is in Christ, He become the example of us and He redeemed all that was lost through the fall of Adam.

*"For He made Him who knew no sin to be sin for us, that we might become the righteousness of God in Him."* (2 Cor 5:21) One man never committed any sin yet He become sin, **it's equally possible to become righteous without committing a single act of righteousness.** Our sins were imputed on Him and He become sin, equally His righteousness has been imputed on us and we have become the righteousness of God in Christ. The word impute is an accounting word which means 'to count on, to put on.' All your sins and my sins and all that happened in Adam was put on Him and it resulted in death. *"The wages of sin is death."* (Rom 6:23)

*"For the love of Christ compels us, because we judge thus: that if One died for all, then all died; and He died for all, that those who live should live no longer for themselves, but for Him who died for them and rose again,"* (2 Cor:14-15). Paul says the love of God compels him not the fear of hell. Many times we preach to scare

people with hell, this was not the motivation of Paul to preach. An exchange took place on the cross, the wages of sin was death, we were to die, Christ took our place, died our death on account of our sins that we may live His life on account of His righteousness. He took your position in death that you may live in His position. Paul concluded *"one has died for all therefore all have died."* All simply means all, not some few believers. As it was in the first Adam all were included and also in the last Adam, Christ, all were included in His death. He died for all that all may live His life. It's easier for many people to believe our inclusion in Adam but we struggle to believe our inclusion in Christ. Christ is the last Adam, as it was in Adam so it is in Christ.

*"Therefore, from now on, we regard no one according to the flesh. Even though we have known Christ according to the flesh, yet now we know Him thus no longer,"* (2 Cor 5:16). Thus Paul concludes he sees no man after the flesh, he recognized something had happened to the entire human race through the death of Christ. All were included in His death. All died and all have been given the privilege to enjoy the life of God if only they can know and believe in what has happened.

In (2 Cor 5:21), He became sin that we may become the righteousness of God in Christ. **Righteousness in not a reward for good behavior**, it is what Christ has done for us. You don't behave good to become righteous, you are righteous first then good behavior follows. Righteousness is a free gift which God has given to us and we ought to receive. *"For if by the one man's offense death reigned through the one, much more those who* *receive abundance of grace and of the gift of righteousness will reign in life through the One, Jesus Christ,"* (Rom 5:17). When you are given a gift by someone, he does not dictate what you do with it, it is yours. Righteousness has been given to us not on account of our performance but as a gift to us, it's only those who receive this gift who reign in life. God does not feel apologetic or intimidated to live in us, He is convinced of what has already happened to us in Christ.

Today righteousness has been classified into two phases, they call it positional righteousness and practical righteousness. They say we are righteous positionally but we have to work out practical righteousness. Paul addresses this issue, *"for they being ignorant of God's righteousness* (positional as they call it)*, and seeking to establish their own righteousness* (practical as they say)*, have not submitted to the righteousness of God."* (Romans 10:3)

Trying to establish our own righteousness we fail to receive the gift of righteousness, it's either you are righteous by faith or not at all, there is nothing like practical righteousness. **Righteousness has never been and will never be a reward for good behavior.** Wow, I know there are many who are having questions over this statement. Have you seen people who are very well behaved but know nothing about Christ? That kind of behavior does not make anyone righteous in God's eyes. God knows only one righteousness which is of Christ and all who have identified themselves with Him enjoy this righteousness.

**Likeness.**

The word righteousness comes from the Anglo Saxon word, "rightwiseness," wise in that which is right. In Greek it comes from the word Dikaios from the root word Dike, it means 'two parties finding a likeness in each other without any feeling inferior or disadvantaged to the other.' God has found a resemblance in man just as it was in the beginning when God made man in His image and likeness.

We have become like Him, we are righteous. He found likeness in Adam and could comfortably identify and fellowship with him. **Likeness is the basis of intimacy**; it's abnormal for humans to become intimate with beasts. God has become intimate with man, He has come to dwell in me and in you.

In Hebrew the word righteousness comes from the word Tzadok. It refers to 'a beam of balance (scale) when two identical weights placed on opposite sides of the scale balance each other.' **We have attained the same weight as God and therefore you are righteous**. When God is on one side of the scale only one that carries His image and likeness can balance Him. That is you and me.

We have tried many gimmicks to become righteous by our own efforts, we still carry the Old Testament mentality of the Pharisees which requires working out our righteousness. The common verse has been (Phil 2:12-13), where Paul speaks of working out your salvation with fear and trembling. In reality Paul states that it is God who works in us to will and to do, so it takes away our self efforts, it is God who works both the will and the doing, not your efforts. I remember my own experience trying to become righteous by obeying the law. I was told the beatitudes in (Matt 5) were a spiritual ladder to reach God and spiritual maturity. I tried and always found myself failing even to climb the first seven steps to reach the first floor yet there were three floors one had to climb to. I tried much harder but could not make it. I was told unless my righteousness overcomes the righteousness of the Pharisees I could not enter heaven. You know the Pharisees fasted twice every week and paid all their tithes. I fasted three times every week just to surpass the Pharisees until my immune system went down and I was attacked by tuberculosis.

The most difficult time for me was when I finished three months without going to church, it seemed to me God had completely given up on me, I was full of guilt, I regretted why I become a Christian because this life was very difficult. I had read many books by great preachers and they all advocated we had to pay a price for God to use us. The greater the price, the greater the glory. I thought my fasting and praying should have qualified me, it was a real difficult moment in my life.

Surprisingly I discovered something unique, for those three months I could not spend in night prayers and fasting my heart was full of peace and comfort. I could not understand how possible this could be, because all along I knew I could only have peace after spending time in prayer and fasting. I began discovering the grace of God. I remember when I was strong enough to go back to church for night prayers, God could use me greatly, I witnessed supernatural move of God in our night meetings, people were getting slain in the Spirit and the gifts of the Spirit were manifesting greatly without fasting because I was still under medication. I could not fast, yet God moved greatly and I understood there was something called grace which I knew nothing about though I was preaching it. This is what Christ paid for that we should enjoy. God does not love us because of what we have done but in-spite of what we have done.

God does not need your righteousness which comes by your efforts, He calls it filthy rags. He has taken His righteousness and given to us as a gift. It is always human desire to see that he has participated in whatever he wants. Many will give testimonies how they received blessings or healing after they had done something, either gave some money or fasted. Yes it may happen because even the old covenant of performance had some glory though it was fading. But that is not God's will for us, God wants us to trust in His finished work and enjoy the results of it manifested in our lives. You only have to receive, *"for all of God's promises have been fulfilled in Christ with a resounding "Yes!" And through Christ, our "Amen" (which means "Yes") ascends to God for his glory."* (2 Cor 1:20, NLT)

We often compete among ourselves who is righteous than the other and often we think if we pray more or fast more or read the Bible more or attend many Christian meetings we become more righteous. That is religious deception. **None of us is more righteous than the other,** you can be more godly than your brother in Christ (more God conscious), but not more righteous.

We have all received the same righteousness which is of Christ and is same to all of us. Stop wasting your energy trying to out do one another, realize you have received a gift of righteousness from God.

*"Moreover the law entered that the offense might abound. But where sin abounded, grace abounded much more, so that as sin reigned in death, even so grace might reign through righteousness to eternal life through Jesus Christ our Lord"* (Rom 5:20-21). Sin reigned through death, grace reigns when we discover how righteous we have become in Christ. When we discover how righteous we have become in Christ we empower God's grace in our lives. The knowledge and consciousness of righteousness empowers us to walk in righteousness.

The devil will always want you to doubt if you are righteous and will keep reminding you of your past mistakes or most recent mistakes to make you doubt your standing before God. He will keep you condemned always trying to work out a righteousness based on behavior modification. We must be aware of the devils schemes and walk in the righteousness we have received by faith in Christ. Any time the devil reminds you of your failure or past sins, declare you are righteous in Christ. The Holy Spirit has no business convicting us of sin. In (John 16:8) the Holy Spirit convicts the world of sin not believers, we are not of the world, we belong to Him and our sins have been completely wiped away. We allow the devil to put condemnation in our minds and we mistake it for the Holy Spirit.

Every morning you wake up, thank God for making you righteous, face the day knowing you are righteous. Many Christians think they are sinners and they face the day trying to become righteous, they fall into many traps of the devil trying to prove to them they are still sinners, they end up confused and condemned and the cycle continues every day. Walk with the knowledge of righteousness by faith not behavior modification.

When you walked in sin, you were a prisoner of sin, your good behavior could not remove you from the prison of sin and make you righteous. When you believed in Christ and received the gift of righteousness by faith you became a prisoner of righteousness, your good or bad behavior can not remove you from this prison because it never brought you in. You are a prisoner of righteousness in Christ. Any one who has this knowledge will never continue in sin, grace teaches you to say no to ungodliness and worldly lusts. We will discuss in details concerning behavior in the chapters ahead, grace is not a license to sin. Paul was accused of the same and had to write a whole chapter in Romans 6 why we should not walk in sin.

**When Christ became sin He never had to do more sin in order to be sin, He automatically became sin through imputed sin.** Likewise when you become the righteousness of God in Christ you need not to add some works to make you more righteous, you are already righteous. When Christ became sin for us, He identified with the human cry *"my God, My God, why have you forsaken me."* God did not forsake Him but He cried the cry man always cries (John 16:32). It caused the Son to go through the most terrible physical and spiritual suffering beyond our human imagination, His face was marred beyond recognition, He was stripped bitterly, His back was like a ploughed land, He was mocked and carried all our diseases, He was chastised for our peace, He died a physical death.

If imputed sin, not committed sin could cause such immense suffering how much more should we expect imputed and imparted righteousness to cause in our lives? It must cause God's life to reign and manifest through us. We ought to experience all of God in us. Abundant joy, love, peace, blessings, success, prosperity, health, wealth should be our portion. **Righteousness simply means it is your right to become all that God is**. He legally became all that you were on the cross that you may become all that He is. *"As He is so are we in this world."* (1 John 4:17). Remember, not as He was, but as He is right now glorified at God's right hand so are we in this world.

When Christ became sin on the cross, He never asked God to send sufferings to Him, He never did anything extra to attract the wrath of God on sin. Automatically things changed, pain and suffering followed Him. Likewise when we become the righteousness of God in Christ we have to do nothing to attract God's favor and blessings, that righteousness will automatically draw the blessings of God to us. It will automatically also draw enemies who are out to oppose us as they opposed Christ.

In His earthly ministry, Christ went round doing good. *"How God anointed Jesus of Nazareth with the Holy Spirit and with power, who went about doing good and healing all who were oppressed by the devil, for God was with Him."* (Acts 10:38). He did a lot of good works, He went round healing all who were oppressed by demons, He fed the hungry, He cleansed the lepers, He taught God's Word to multitudes. None of the good works He had done was considered at the cross but faced all the judgment on sin. His sentence was not reduced on account of good works because all my bad works were also imputed on Him and His good works were imputed on us. *"For we are His workmanship, created in Christ Jesus for good works, which God prepared beforehand that we should walk in them."* (Eph 2:10). His good works were ordained for you to walk in them, God worked it all before that you should not struggle manifesting His life.

God took His good works and deposited them on your account, you need to withdraw them and manifest them through the Spirit who lives in us. **Your account is already full of good works on account of Christ's good works, withdraw them and manifest them.** Don't bring in your own works of straw or wood, the complete works of gold are already there, manifest them. It is God who causes us to will and to do His good works. It is a finished work, God never left out some homework for you, He finished it all, yours is to rely on His Spirit to enjoy all that belongs to you. *"Let us be glad and rejoice, and give honor to him: for the marriage of the lamb is come, and his wife has made herself ready. And to her it was granted that she should be arrayed in fine* *linen, clean and white: for the fine linen is the righteousness of the saints."* (Rev. 19:7-8. AV)

The reason why Christ went through all that sufferings was not for Himself or His own benefit, He went through it all for me and for you. He became sin that you be righteous, He become a curse that you be blessed, all sicknesses were put on Him that you should walk in wholeness, became poor for our riches, rejected and despised that you may be accepted, stripped that you may be healed, why do we behave as if this did not take place, as if God is still waiting for us to do something extra to enjoy the benefits of the cross? That is a lie of religion, religion prides when we go round in circles trying to get what we already have received, as Andrew Wommack puts it, 'it's like a dog chasing its own tail.' Christ declared all the Father has are His and when the Holy Spirit comes He will take that which belongs to Christ and declare it to us (John 16:15). All He went through was for you, enjoy this without strings attached.

When God created Adam and Eve, He covered them with His glory that they couldn't notice they were naked, they were so innocent. Immediately after they partook the forbidden fruit which I do believe its the devil who put it there, they discovered they were naked and ashamed, initially they were naked and unashamed. They began to make some covering of leaves. This represents man's best works trying to restore the glory of God in his life, trying to cover the nakedness brought by the knowledge of sin which causes us to run far from God as Adam did. Adam's covering could not lust, God calls our righteous works filthy rags.

He made a covering for Adam and his spouse of animal skin, which was a picture of the sacrificial system which also was a temporary cover. It never restored the glory of God, it never restored the innocence of man. Under the old system sacrifices only covered sins but never removed sins. Christ offered the perfect sacrifice which removed sins once for all and restored the glory of God over mankind. We are no-longer naked, we don't need to cover ourselves with our works to impress God, no. *"Those who have been baptized into Christ have put on Christ"* (Gal 3:27). That's the perfect garment that restored God's glory over us as it was in Adam.

In this higher life which God has called us to live, the only currency that works is faith. We have to believe what God says, right believing will produce the right results. Can you imagine prince Charles heir to the throne of the British monarchy not believing that he is the prince? You could dress him and teach him how to behave like a prince and even force him to live in the Buckingham palace but he will not stay there for long because he does not believe he is the prince. You will find him in the streets of London behaving like a common citizen of Britain. What makes him behave like a prince? He fully knows and fully believes he is the prince and heir to the throne. Many of us today do not manifest the life of God because we are not sure who we are, We don't believe we are righteous, we need to add something extra and improve our behavior to feel we are qualified to be righteous.

## Highway

*"A highway shall be there, and a road, and it shall be called the Highway of Holiness. The unclean shall not pass over it, but it shall be for others. Whoever walks the road, although a fool, Shall not go astray."* (Isaiah 35:8). Isaiah sees a highway of holiness, the unclean shall not walk in it. All those who want to attain righteousness by their own efforts apart from Christ will not walk in it. And those who have appropriated Christ's righteousness in their lives even if they are fools will walk in it without going astray because it does not require their efforts. A highway has a capacity to accommodate many vehicles in different lanes moving on the same direction at high speeds. In a highway all obstacles which may hinder the free flow of vehicles on the same direction have been removed. Vehicles from opposing directions do not meet in a highway. Isaiah sees a highway with a capacity to carry many of us, all obstacles removed for us to move along well.

**Holiness is nolonger an exclusive club of a few men of God who can fast for forty days and a few bishops but it's a high way with a capacity to carry all of us** who have received the free-gift of righteousness in Christ Jesus. Holiness is the life of God which manifests through us on the platform of us accepting God's righteousness. The righteousness by faith in Christ has qualified us to walk in holiness as God. We have been set apart by the Holy Spirit who is the guarantee of our inheritance. The Holy Spirit by virtue of living in us has sanctified us to be holy. In the Old Testament wherever God dwelt was declared holy,

God dwells in us and has made us to be holy as He is. The scriptures refers to us as a holy nation, royal priesthood, (1 Pet 2:9), holy brothers, (Heb 3:1), holy temple (1 Cor 3:17). You can not claim to be holy when you are working out your own righteousness by works, this is what religion does today, we refuse the gift of righteousness by faith and claim we are holy. Many students in monasteries have been taught to try hard and walk in holiness yet they don't understand anything about righteousness by faith.

A man was taking a voyage a cross the pacific, his name was Andrew. Andrew got a sponsorship after a long time of trying, the sponsor paid his ticket for the journey. Andrew was grateful but not exited about his trip, at the back of his mind he had an obstacle to overcome, he never knew how he will feed himself and pay for other services during the voyage. He knew the ticket only covered the transportation costs. Throughout this journey Andrew could wait for people to be served with food and then go for the left-overs. He never went to the dinning hall for food because he thought he could be asked to pay for the meals. In many instances he had to volunteer to do the dishes in the kitchen just to get some left-overs.

The man struggled a lot during this voyage; he never enjoyed the swimming pool, the games, the movies, the soft drinks and the variety of meals which were offered on board. The voyage was to take three weeks. One night one of the workers in the ship who had observed Andrew for sometime approached him and asked why he never ate with the rest of the passengers, why he never enjoyed the games, the movies and the other available services. Andrew told him he had no money to pay for his meals let alone the others.

He asked him for his ticket, at the back of the ticket there was a stamp which read 'all paid.' This worker told Andrew, when the ticket was paid all was included, the meals, the entertainments, the drinks, laundry services and everything he could have desired to enjoy on board. Andrew was stunned, for two and a half weeks he was barely surviving onboard yet all was paid for. From that day he enjoyed everything which was entitled to him on board the ship.

We need to realize when we believed in Christ we received all, we were justified, sanctified, glorified, we received the gift of righteousness, blessings, curses broken, we were made holy, we received good works in our account (only our bodies wait for glorification). There is no need to starve ourselves waiting to enjoy in heaven what has been paid for us to enjoy in this life, when all has been included in Christ. 1 Cor 2:12 tells us *"we have received the Spirit who is from God that we may know the things freely given to us."* Do you know them or you are busy working for them? We have nothing to work out, it is all included in Christ. There will be weeping in heaven not because of joy of getting into heaven but because we will discover all that belonged to us but we failed to enjoy. Paul says *"the present sufferings can not be compared with the glory that shall be revealed in us,"* (Rom 8:18, KJV). The glory is already in you.

*"The voice of one crying in the wilderness: "Prepare the way of the LORD; Make straight in the desert a highway for our God. Every valley shall be exalted and every mountain and hill brought low; the crooked places shall be made straight and the rough places smooth,"* (Isaiah 40:3-4). Every excuse men had for not living the life of God have been removed. The rough places have been made smooth, the crooked places have been made straight, the valleys have been exalted and the mountains and hills have been brought low. A way has been made for us to experience the original, intended life of God for man, we are walking in the highway of the Lord. This has been the desire of God and now it has been fulfilled.

**Every excuse which man had has been remove**d. The law and its commandments, sin and its power on the human flesh have all been conclusively dealt with on the cross of Christ. You are righteous, you are partaker of the divine nature, you are a participant in the life of God, you are God's righteousness in Christ, and God has found a dwelling in you. He has come with everything, He is in your life. Enjoy this life without feeling intimidated, God has found a likeness in you. God's testimony is greater than man's testimony.

Isaiah 40 begins by leveling the ground, a runway is prepared for the Lord. It ends by those who wait upon the Lord, (Wait in Hebrew KAWVA) "intertwined" with the Lord mounting up with wings. The best result of walking on this runway will always be to fly high with the Lord.

# FIVE

## OUR INCLUSION IN CHRIST

One unique thing that separates Christianity from other faiths is the emblem of the cross, it's surprising that the cross which was used by the Romans as an instrument of execution many years ago has become the emblem of the Christian faith. The cross was not an invention of the Romans, it was in God's mind before creation. All that was done wrong in Adam was made right through the cross of Jesus Christ. Man's origin was not in Adam but in Christ. (Eph 1:4). He chose us in Christ before the foundation of the world. Before Adam was formed, God already had a picture of us in Christ. The fall of Adam did not interfere with God's plan for humanity. When a picture is damaged what is needed is a negative, you can get the exact picture by processing the negative. Christ was the negative of the true picture of man. Many times we have magnified the fall of Adam as if it destroyed all that God had in mind concerning mankind. **God who has a fore knowledge of all things could have not planned for humanity to have a worst end than his beginning.**

Since the fall of Adam mankind seemed to be hopeless and held in a trap of sin which he could not get himself out. *"Nevertheless death reigned from Adam to Moses, even over those who had not sinned according to the likeness of the transgression of Adam, who is a type of Him who was to come."* (Rom.5:14-15). Through the fall of Adam man stood condemned without hope. Death reigned through all humanity because Adam was our representative. Everything he did wrong we were all included in it. (John 3:17), Christ did not come to condemn the world but save a condemned world. When you visit a prison and find a prisoner who is already condemned to be hanged, condemning him again will not be of any help or will not add him any more punishment, the only thing you can do to make a difference in his life is to remove the condemnation, to get him out of the prison and to cancel the sentence. Christ did exactly that, He did not come to condemn us because already we stood condemned by the fall of Adam, He could only save us by taking our place of condemnation.

## The Incarnation

God in His fore knowledge was aware of what will become of man through Adam, **He designed the human body with a full awareness that He was in future to put on the human body**. He designed the human body with a capacity for all the fullness of God to fit in. Man's union with God is the original thought that inspired creation. Man has been made with a capacity to carry the divine. Because mans' origin was not in Adam, when Adam fell God went back to the blue print of man, the original authentic picture of man to redeem the fallen image. Christ come in place of the first Adam, Just as the first Adam represented mankind in all aspects, Christ the last Adam represented man in the same capacity in all aspects. He swallowed humanity in Himself.

In the fullness of time, a virgin conceived of the Holy Spirit, the seed which had been promised back in Eden. Mary gives birth to a

Son who is to redeem the image and likeness of God in man. The Word that was from the beginning that stood face to face with God, that made all things and without Him nothing was made that existed, He humbled Himself and partook the human body. The bearer of the image and the likeness of God stepped into the planet earth in a human suit. His birth divides history into a before and after, our calender communicates an event which took place 2000 years ago. It is easier to imagine Jesus at thirty years of age fully grown, walking the streets of Jerusalem doing miracles, healing and preaching to people.

But it is so difficult to imagine Jesus as a child completely dependent on human parents for everything yet He made all things. As a one day or one week or one month old baby, His survival was completely in the hands of His human parents. This is real humility without contradiction. He tasted the full cycle of human life from womb to tomb. He fully identified with humanity. *"And the Word became flesh and dwelt among us, and we beheld His glory, the glory as of the only begotten of the Father, full of grace and truth."* (John 1:14). Listen to this, *"suddenly the invisible eternal Word takes on 'visible form! The incarnation! In him and now confirmed in us! The most accurate tangible display of God's eternal thought finds expression in human life! The Word become a human being; we are his address: he resides in us! He captivates our gaze! The glory we see there is not a religious replica; he is the authentic begotten son. The Glory (that Adam lost) returns in fullness! Only grace can communicate truth in such complete context."* (Mirror trans)

God has made Himself so much visible and comprehensible to man by taking the form of a human being, Had He come to us as an angel He could have remained a mystery to us, but by putting on the human body and becoming like us He Has made Himself so visible, so real to us. Separation from God has always been an illusion, all of creation is contained in Him. God is Emmanuel to us. When God became man, He was not visiting His creation but came to stay. By Christ taking the form of man, He completely changed His status and the next time we see Him we shall see Him in a human glorified body, we shall be like Him. **We have a man sitting at the throne room of heaven.**

When God became man He fully identified with all that man is. He was empowered by the Holy Spirit at His baptism for ministry, *"And Jesus, when he was baptized, went up straightway out of the water: and, lo, the heavens were opened unto him, and he saw the Spirit of God descending like a dove, and lighting upon him."* (Matt 3:16). You don't empower God for ministry only man needs empowerment.

At His greatest hour of distress an angel of God had to strengthen Him, *"Then an angel appeared to Him from heaven, strengthening Him."* (Luke 22:43). If He had not fully become man, He couldn't have needed an angel to strengthen Him, you can not strengthen God. He tested death like any human being. *"And when Jesus had cried out with a loud voice, He said, "Father, 'into Your hands I commit My spirit.'" Having said this, He breathed His last."* (Luke 23:46). He received authority from

God, "And Jesus came and spoke to them, saying, *"All authority has been given to Me in heaven and on earth."* (Matt 28:18). He received Man's re-inherited authority which Adam had lost, you can not give God authority. He was fully man.

## Mirror, mirror

Christ the example of us steps into the human body, Him who made all things humbled Himself to partake a human body. *"He came into the very world he created, but the world didn't recognize him. He came to his own people, and even they rejected him."* (John 1:10-11, NLT). Imagine being away for a long time you come back home, you can recognize every persons' face but unfortunately they don't remember you, they don't recognize you. Everything He did He did in my name, He was not the example for me to copy from but the example of the perfect me. He came to reveal man's identity and to redeem it. He revealed our identify as it was before we lost it in Adam.

We study our Bible as a window shopping material. In window shopping you see what you don't have and admire it, should you have enough money, you buy it and it becomes yours. Should you not afford, you will be left only to admire. We study the scriptures admiring the life of Jesus wishing we could do what He did, we could just be like Him, and we sing songs expressing the same desire yet we fail to realize Christ is the example of you.

When you see the life of Jesus it mirrors you, it mirrors all that man is, the blue print of man, the complete man. He is the mirror reflection of you. Whatever you see written about Him is about you. **The entire Bible is about Jesus and all about Jesus is about you**. See yourself in Christ. If you wish to comprehend what God had in mind by creating man, look at the perfect man Christ. Whatever He did put your name there. It's absurd to see one gazing into a mirror and admiring what he sees and wishes he could have what he sees in the mirror, such a person we could refer to as insane. The mirror only reflects what you already have, the mirror does not create anything it reflects what already is. It shows who we are. Imagine someone taking a mirror and tries to look at his face in darkness, you know the result, he will see nothing. You need light for the mirror to function. Only in God's light are we able to see ourselves in His mirror.

*"But we all, with unveiled face, beholding as in a mirror the glory of the Lord, are being transformed into the same image from glory to glory, just as by the Spirit of the Lord."* (2 Cor 3:18). As we behold Christ the mirror reflection of us we are transformed by this awareness from the glory of the flesh to the glory of God. The Spirit Himself does this, we see and we share in this knowledge of our new identity in Christ. *"Now every single one of us have our faces unveiled with new understanding; the days of window-shopping are over! God has cancelled the times of ignorance! (Acts 17:30) We see ourselves in Him as in a mirror and are restored to radiate the exact same image; we are changed from an inferior mind-set to the revealed opinion of our true origin. This transformation is engineered by the Spirit of the Lord."* (Mirror)

## In my Name

Had He done all the miracles He did and failed to deal with sin, man could still be eternally condemned. We could still be held captive in the disobedience of Adam. *"The next day John saw Jesus coming toward him, and said, "Behold! The Lamb of God who takes away the sin of the world!"* (John 1:29). When John saw Him he recognized Him as the lamb of God who takes away the sin of the world.

We become sinners not by choice but through one man's sin, just as we were included in the fall of Adam so were we included in the obedience of Christ. *"Nevertheless death reigned from Adam to Moses, even over those who had not sinned according to the likeness of the transgression of Adam, who is a type of Him who was to come."* (Rom 5:14). When the devil thought he was dealing with one man, he failed to realize all of us were included in Christ a type of Adam. All my sins were imputed on Him at the cross, He died my death, faced the cross in my name not in His name that I may live His life, (2 Cor 5:15).

(Romans 5:15-19) Paul makes a comparison of what happened in Adam and what happened in Christ. Paul uses the words **much more** repeatedly, much more simply means much more. Water in an ocean is much more than water in a bath tab. If all died in Adam much more are made alive in Christ. Adams fall led to the condemnation of many, much more Christ's obedience leads to the justification of many. Adam's disobedience brought sin and sin brought death, Christ's obedience brought grace to all, righteousness and eternal life (Rom 5:21). He completely reversed the impact of Adam's fall, man shall never be held hostage by what happened in Adam.

*"But God's free gift immeasurably outweighs the transgression. For if through the transgression of the one individual the mass of mankind have died, infinitely greater is the generosity with which God's grace, and the gift given in His grace which found expression in the one man Jesus Christ, have been bestowed on the mass of mankind. And it is not with the gift as it was with the results of one individual's sin; for the judgment which one individual provoked resulted in condemnation, whereas the free gift after a multitude of transgressions results in acquittal. For if, through the transgression of the one individual, Death made use of the one individual to seize the sovereignty, all the more shall those who receive God's overflowing grace and gift of righteousness reign as kings in Life through the one individual, Jesus Christ. It follows then that just as the result of a single transgression is a condemnation which extends to the whole race, so also the result of a single decree of righteousness is a life-giving acquittal which extends to the whole race. For as through the disobedience of the one individual the mass of mankind were constituted sinners, so also through the obedience of the One the mass of mankind will be constituted righteous."* (Rom 5:15-19 Weymouth Trans). **The free gift after much transgression results in acquittal.** The result of a single decree of righteousness is a life giving acquittal which extends to the whole race. That's the impact of the cross of Christ, it carries much more significance than the fall of Adam.

The Kenyan national soccer team plays the Uganda national team, all the stadium is packed with enthusiastic football funs ready to cheer their Kenyan team to victory. The match kicks off and at the 70th minute Dennis a Kenyan striker scores a goal for his side and the entire stadium erupts into jubilation. Immediately the score board reads Kenya 1 Uganda 0. To my amazement the score board does not read Dennis 1 Uganda 0. Dennis was not playing for himself but for Kenya, he was wearing a Kenyan shirt and whatever he did he did on behalf of the nation. The match ends with the same score and the funs can not stop celebrating because they are included in the victory. There is a Kenyan citizen who lives in the remotest parts of lokichogio lokitang, he does not know what happened, he does not know who Dennis is, he does not believe in football, he does not know how to dribble a ball, is he also included in the victory or not? Definitely he is included as long as he is a citizen of Kenya, his unbelief does not change the result of what has happened. He can not enjoy the celebration because of ignorance and unbelief.

In the same manner all of mankind was equally included in the death and resurrection of Jesus Christ. He never died His death but our death, He died in your name. It's unfortunate some of us are 2000 years late to attend their funerals. He never won a victory for Himself but for us. He won victory in your name, the trophy does not have His name on it but your name has been fully engrafted on the trophy. Whether we believe it or not, **our unbelief does not change the results of what already has taken place**. Paul declares, *"the love of God compels us for we have* *come to know that when one died all died"* (2 Cor 5:14). We were all included in this death and this reality compelled Paul to preach. Col 1:17 tells us in Christ all things consist. All of creation consists fully in Him. It's only the believer in Christ who has identified with this reality and reaps the benefits of their inclusion. The good news is in what has already happened in Christ. We should make all men aware of the victory won in their name, they have no reason to be held captive with the lies of the devil.

**Fully Acquitted.**
*"Who was surrendered to death because of the offences we had committed, and was raised to life because of the acquittal secured for us."* (Rom. 4:25, Weymouth translation). He was delivered for our transgression yet He was raised because we were acquitted. The judgment of sin required death, Christ died to sin according to the demand of the law. He went to the cross because of our sins imputed on Him. Sin received its full judgement on the cross not only the sins of Christians but the entire human race. We owe sin nothing. He was raised because the judgment on sin was fully met and man stood acquitted before God. Had He not satisfied judgment on sin He could not have been raised because He never died His own death but our death, His resurrection meant our victory over sin.

On His death He never represented the believers but the entire human race, He satisfied judgment on sin and His resurrection meant only one thing, **judgment for sin was fully satisfied and man who was guilty now stands acquitted**. The innocence of man before the fall has fully been restored. If Jesus took your place in a court of judgement and He stood trial for you, if He was convicted and served the sentence and finally was released it only meant one thing. You are free. You can walk free without fear of being arrested and charged for the crime, the case is closed. The case for your sins has been closed. *"He was looked down on and passed over, a man who suffered, who knew pain firsthand. One look at him and people turned away. We looked down on him, thought he was scum. But the fact is, it was our pains he carried—our disfigurements, all the things wrong with us. We thought he brought it on himself, that God was punishing him for his own failures. But it was our sins that did that to him, that ripped and tore and crushed him—our sins! He took the punishment, and that made us whole. Through his bruises we get healed."* (Isaiah 53:3-5, Message translation). Everything wrong about man was put on Him at the cross. Every sickness, diseases, curses, poverty, disorders, sins, whatever was wrong with man He dealt with.

*"Still, it's what GOD had in mind all along, to crush him with pain. The plan was that he give himself as an offering for sin so that he'd see life come from it—life, life, and more life. And GOD's plan will deeply prosper through him. Out of that terrible travail of soul, he'll see that it's worth it and be glad he did it. Through what he experienced, my righteous one, my servant, will make many "righteous ones," as he himself carries the burden of their sins. Therefore I'll reward him extravagantly—the best of everything, the highest honors—because he looked death in the*

*face and didn't flinch, because he embraced the company of the lowest. He took on his own shoulders the sin of the many, he took up the cause of all the black sheep."* (Isaiah 53:10-12, Message translation) He himself carried the burden for our sins and it was worth, it resulted in us being made righteous. In the mind of God judgment on sin was fully met and mans' innocence was restored. Now it's upon man to hear this good news and put his faith in it, believe in the report that God has given about his acquittal, his unbelief will keep him away from what has taken place. God tells Peter, **"What God has cleansed you must not call common."** (Acts 10:15).

Man is no longer unclean, the blood has dealt with our sins. Paul addressing a group of Greek philosophers who were idol worshipers, he tells them *"though He is not far from each one of us; "for in Him we live and move and have our being, as also some of your own poets have said, 'For we are also His offspring."* (Acts 17: 27-28). Mankind is not the property of the devil. A thief may keep a stolen property for as long as he can but it will never become his, when he is found, he will have to restore the stolen property.

I like using this example of developing a negative to get the full picture. Christ the negative of the true human picture went to the cross to develop what we lost through Adam. For three hours when Christ was on that cross, there was complete darkness. The negative was in the dark room processing the image and likeness of God which had been hidden and distorted by sin. Did he succeed? Yes, He succeeded in redeeming the original design of man. Now what stands before man is the tree of life, Jesus the life giver, man has to believe in Jesus and receive this life eternal purposed for us.

"But Jesus answered them saying, *"The hour has come that the son of man should be glorified. "Most assuredly, I say to you, unless the grain of wheat fall into the ground and dies, it remains alone, but if it dies it produces much grain. "* (John 12:23-24). This is the product of the cross. Get this, a fruit is ripe when the seed in the fruit equals the seed that was sown in the ground.

A story is told of a slave owner who kept many slaves in his farm in Brazil, at that time slavery was still legal. After a long campaign for the abolishment of slave trade, it was finally agreed that slavery should come to an end in Brazil and a date was set for all slaves to be set free by their owners. This news was published in the newspapers. This particular slave owner got a copy of the paper and he hid it from his slaves. None of the slaves knew that a date had been set for the release of all slaves, they continued working even after the set date. One time, this slave owner was sick and bed ridden, he called in one of his trusted slaves to take care of him in his house. While attending to his master he came across a newspaper which had set a date for the release of the slaves in Brazil. To his surprise, it was three years ago when the date set by the state expired. He was so shocked, for three years they had been working illegally as slaves without the knowledge of the state. Slavery had been abolished three years ago.

The slave rushed out of the room and called all the other slaves and showed them the newspaper, he read it to all of them, there was great jubilation in that farm. When the slave owner heard the noise, he struggled out of his bed to see what had happened to his slaves. To his surprise he saw them carrying a newspaper and shouting freedom, immediately he realized his lies had come to an end and he could not keep the slaves anymore, they had discovered their freedom. That day all the slaves packed and left for good, he could not order for their arrest as he could do before. That newspaper was the evidence of their freedom.

**The body of Jesus on the cross was the document of mans' guilt. His resurrection was the receipt for mans' acquittal.** It is the evidence that the sacrifice for our sins was received and accepted and that man is no longer guilty in God's face. *"His body nailed to the cross hung there as the document of mankind's guilt, in dying our death he deleted the detailed hand written record of Adam's fall. Every stain that sin left on our conscience was fully blotted out."* (Col 2:14, Mirror)

The devil has no right to hold us in bondage to sin any more. When the lamb was slain in Egypt, all the Jews were set free from the bondage of Pharaoh, Pharaoh was totally defeated but they had to put their faith in God individually in the wilderness to enter the promised land. The resurrection of Christ meant victory to the entire human race but man has to individually believe in Christ to enjoy the fruit of redemption. The devil knows this well and he has employed our ignorance to keep us from enjoying the fruit of redemption. The first time you hear this message always there will be someone trying to dismiss this, but the moment you grasp this truth, the devil knows you are off his hook.

## Sin Dethroned

Sin had the human body as its base of operation, it had total control and authority of the human body, even though the law demanded what was good for man, it was weakened by sins dominance in the human flesh. Christ took on Himself the human body to judge sin in its domain. *"Therefore, when He came into the world, He said: "Sacrifice and offering You did not desire, But a body You have prepared for Me."* ( Heb. 10:5). It had to be done in the human body.

*"For the law of the Spirit of life in Christ Jesus has made me free from the law of sin and death. For what the law could not do in that it was weak through the flesh, God did by sending His own Son in the likeness of sinful flesh, on account of sin: He condemned sin in the flesh, that the righteous requirement of the law might be fulfilled in us who do not walk according to the flesh but according to the Spirit."* (Rom. 8:2-4).

Christ condemned sin in the human body satisfying the judgment on sin at the cross, He dethroned sin from its domain in the human flesh and sin no longer has the right to hold us captive. It was fully judged in the human flesh. The New Living translation puts it very clear *"the Law of Moses was unable to save us because of the weakness of our sinful nature. So God did what the law could not do. He sent his own Son in a body like the bodies we sinners have. And in that body **God declared an end to sin's control over us by***

**giving his Son as a sacrifice for our sins.** *He did this so that the just requirement of the law would be fully satisfied for us..."* (Rom 8:3-4). Sin has fully been judged in its territory, it has been dethroned of the authority to operate in human flesh. You can live the life of God without being captive to sin.

*"Sin can't tell you how to live. After all, you're not living under that old tyranny any longer. You're living in the freedom of God. So, since we're out from under the old tyranny, does that mean we can live any old way we want? Since we're free in the freedom of God, can we do anything that comes to mind? Hardly. You know well enough from your own experience that there are some acts of so-called freedom that destroy freedom. Offer yourselves to sin, for instance, and it's your last free act. But offer yourselves to the ways of God and the freedom never quits. All your lives you've let sin tell you what to do. But thank God you've started listening to a new master, one whose commands set you free to live openly in his freedom! But now that you've found you don't have to listen to sin tell you what to do, and have discovered the delight of listening to God telling you, what a surprise! A whole, healed, put-together life right now, with more and more of life on the way!"* (Rom. 6:14-18, 22. Message trans)

We can no longer be held captive by the fall of Adam, Adams sin received full judgment at the cross of Christ when He who knew no sin, who never had any sin or did any sin become sin that we may become the righteousness of God in Christ Jesus but unfortunately man has not known this. *"You were in Christ when He died which means that **His death represents your true*** *circumcision*. *Sin's authority in the human body was stripped off you in Him dying your death.*" (Col 2:11, Mirror)

Christ died our death, judged sin in our human body, satisfied judgment on sin, faced the devil in our name not His name and overcame the devil as a man not as God. His victory was our victory, His success was our success but ignorance has kept us from enjoying this. *"Having disarmed principalities and powers, He made a public spectacle of them, triumphing over them in it."* (Col. 2:15) He disarmed the devil in my name, the devil was defeated by a man born of a woman and that's why it is his joy to keep men under captivity due to their ignorance. Ignorance empowers an already defeated enemy.

The Weymouth translation paints a picture of the whole encounter. *"And the hostile princes and rulers He shook off from Himself, and boldly displayed them as His conquests, when by the Cross He triumphed over them."* (Col 2:15). The devil had taken Jesus captive as a prisoner of sin, He died a sinners death, received by demons and was being forced to bow before the devil. He shook them off from Himself, the devil fell before Him, He stepped on his head and crushed the serpents head, disarming him, taking the keys of death and hades and made a triumphal parade of the devil before all his demons.

In the ancient Roman tradition, when the Romans defeated an enemy, they chopped off his thumbs and big toes so that he could not hold a weapon. They removed from him his royal garments and any ornaments which made him look great. They tied him to a chariot or a horse, dragged him, marching him naked before their citizens and mocking him so that none of them will ever live under fear of that enemy. They all proved that the enemy was truly defeated. This is what Christ did to the devil. He made a public spectacle of a defeated foe. God raised Him up after securing an eternal redemption for us. He was delivered because of our transgressions and was raised because we were justified. (Rom. 4:25). When He was raised we were co-raised with Him. (Eph 2:5). See yourself seated with Christ.

God gave Him a name above all names *"And being found in appearance as a man, He humbled Himself and became obedient to the point of death, even the death of the cross. Therefore God also has highly exalted Him and given Him the name which is above every name,"* (Phil. 2:8-9).

**Fully Reconciled**
God has become Emmanuel to every human being, He has reconciled Himself to us. *"Now all things are of God, who has reconciled us to Himself through Jesus Christ, and has given us the ministry of reconciliation, that is, that God was in Christ reconciling the world to Himself, not imputing their trespasses to them, and has committed to us the word of reconciliation. Now then, we are ambassadors for Christ, as though God were pleading through us: we implore you on Christ's behalf, be reconciled to God."* (2 Cor.5:18-20). Jesus did not come to reconcile God back to His creation, He came to reconcile the world back to God, God has never been separated from His

creation, in Him we live, move and have our beings, He fills the heaven and earth. Its us who have been running away from Him, sin separated man from God not God from man, we were enemies in our minds, we conceived a guilty conscience (Col 1:20-21). Finally He has reconciled us back to Himself.

Through the cross He dealt with sin, not imputing sin on us, because He imputed sin on Christ, sin faced judgement on the body of Christ. You can't punish one offense twice, if Christ bore the punishment for my sins then I won't be punished for the same again. God has reconciled his creation through the event on the cross. He has called us to be ambassadors for reconciliation. Tell the world they have been reconciled, they should change their minds and stop running away. Christianity is not about God who is in a bad mood who we must try and persuaded to change His mood, but a God who has already reconciled Himself to His creation. He has done all that was possible to give man victory and restore us to our original identity. *"I have been found by those who were not looking for Me, I have revealed Myself to those who were not inquiring of Me. "* (Rom 10:20, WEY)

He says in Revelation 3:20, " He stands at the door and knock and if any man hears and opens the door He will come in and dine with them." Which door is He standing at, His door or your door? God has moved from His door and is standing boldly knocking at the door of your heart. He has come, He is hear, closer to you than your breath, not only to believers but to the unbeliever. Paul tells the unbelievers in Mars hill, God is not far from any of them (Acts 17:27). God believed in their salvation even before they were born and paid the price for their sins. **It is not about man's best lamb to draw God near but God's own initiative.** If sin were greater than God's love then redemption could be impossible. Through His love which is difficult to comprehend with human understanding He reconciled us to Himself. He justly judged sin at the cross of Christ. The devil can not reverse the cross but can employ our ignorance. The sacrifice on the cross was not consumed by God's anger as was Elijah's sacrifice. It was big enough to satisfy God's wrath on sin.

# *SIX*

## FORGIVENESS OF SIN

One commodity which has for along time found its place in the Christian circles and fetched lot's of praise has been guilt. It has been marketed in our churches to the pleasure of the devil. In fact some preachers measure the impact of their messages by how guilty the congregation feels after every preaching. The way to get people come back to church next Sunday has been to make them feel God is not happy with them, they should do something to make God happy. They should always feel they owe God something. The church has greatly borrowed from the Roman Catholic dark age years where people had to do things to earn God's forgiveness. Guilt was a common product in the pulpit of the church marketed to the congregations. Repentance was interpreted as penance or indulgence, which meant paying for forgiveness. Indulgence was sold to the congregation and people could even pay for the sins they were yet to commit or for their relatives who were assumed to be in purgatory. This guilt money was used to put up the big cathedrals which today have turned into museums in Europe. We have not fully grasped the extent of the liberation which the blood of Christ secured for us.

A man once owed his friend a lot of money, he could not feel free to face this friend, any time he saw him coming he could hide himself, wherever they were together he felt so intimidated because of the debt which he could not pay. He never enjoyed the fellowship of this friend not because the friend would ask him to pay him back, no, he always felt indebted. One of his friends realized this and settled the bill for him without his knowledge. He still behaved the same wherever he saw the lender. One day the lender told him he need not be worried about the bill, it was settled, he felt very much relieved, he could fellowship with this friend without any intimidation because the bill had been settled. We cannot enjoy fellowship with God as long as we feel we are indebted to Him, **any real fellowship must have no room for one partner feeling inferior or indebted or else it will be manipulation**.

Our Lord's Prayer has formed the basis of all this confusion today in the church. *"In this manner, therefore, pray: Our Father in heaven, Hallowed be Your name. Your kingdom come. Your will be done On earth as it is in heaven. Give us this day our daily bread. And forgive us our debts, As we forgive our debtors. And do not lead us into temptation, But deliver us from the evil one. For Yours is the kingdom and the power and the glory forever. Amen. "For if you forgive men their trespasses, your heavenly Father will also forgive you. "But if you do not forgive men their trespasses, neither will your Father forgive your trespasses."* (Matt 6:9-15)

This prayer by all means looks a very sincere prayer but it has a lot which do not relate with the New Testament. With the reality of incarnation and the indwelling Spirit of God in us, we can not wish for the kingdom to come, the kingdom already is within us, the Father is within us through His Spirit who lives in us. The forgiveness promised is a conditional forgiveness, **to the degree you forgive you will be forgiven**, if you forgive 30% you will be forgiven 30%. This is a typical teaching designed to discourage the people who would seek justification by their efforts. This is an Old Testament prayer.

The New Testament sets a completely different precedence, Paul says *"bearing with one another, and forgiving one another, if anyone has a complaint against another; even as Christ forgave you, so you also must do."* ( Col 3:13).

*"And be kind to one another, tenderhearted, forgiving one another, just as God in Christ forgave you."* (Eph 4:32). *"And you, being dead in your trespasses and the uncircumcision of your flesh, He has made alive together with Him, having forgiven you all trespasses,"* (Col 2:13). Forgiveness under the New Testament is not conditional. We have been forgiven unconditionally and we forgive not to be forgiven but because we have been forgiven, we extend what we have received to others. Let's picture into these truths which indicate a difference between the old system and the consequences of the new system in regard to forgiveness of sins.

### Covenant Changed

The writer of Hebrews paints a clear picture to us of what used to happen under the old covenant and what happened through Christ. He reveals the weaknesses of the old covenant and why God had to initiate another covenant.

*"For if that first covenant had been faultless, then no place would have been sought for a second. Because finding fault with them, He says: "Behold, the days are coming, says the LORD, when I will make a new covenant with the house of Israel and with the house of Judah— "not according to the covenant that I made with their fathers in the day when I took them by the hand to lead them out of the land of Egypt; because they did not continue in My covenant, and I disregarded them, says the LORD. "For this is the covenant that I will make with the house of Israel after those days, says the LORD: I will put My laws in their mind and write them on their hearts; and I will be their God, and they shall be My people. "None of them shall teach his neighbor, and none his brother, saying, 'Know the LORD,' for all shall know Me, from the least of them to the greatest of them. "For I will be merciful to their unrighteousness, and their sins and their lawless deeds I will remember no more." In that He says, "A new covenant," He has made the first obsolete. Now what is becoming obsolete and growing old is ready to vanish away."* (Heb. 8:7- 13).

In this New Testament, God declares He will be merciful to our unrighteousness, our sins and iniquities He will not remember. We read this scripture many times, I wonder whether we really get the meaning of it. It clearly says it's not like the old covenant where a record of wrongs was kept. In this testament He has become merciful to our unrighteousness. **Our sins and lawless deeds He will remember no more, not today and not in the future.** Not at the point of confession but on the basis of this testament, He will never at any moment hold us guilty of sin, He has no more memory of my sin.

When a covenant is changed there must of necessity be a change of the law also, you can not operate a new covenant with laws of a previous covenant. The priesthood was changed from Levitical priesthood to the priesthood of Christ who is from the house of Judah. *"For the priesthood being changed, of necessity there is also a change of the law. For He of whom these things are spoken belongs to another tribe, from which no man has officiated at the altar. For it is evident that our Lord arose from Judah, of which tribe Moses spoke nothing concerning priesthood. And it is yet far more evident if, in the likeness of Melchizedek, there arises another priest, "* (Heb 7:12-15).

With the change of priesthood also comes the change in the operations of the priest and consequently a change in the accomplishments. We can not expect the same results which were under the previous covenant to be in this one. If the former did not take away sins, this new one accomplished that.

### Eternal Spirit

*"It was symbolic for the present time in which both gifts and sacrifices are offered which cannot make him who performed the service perfect in regard to the conscience— concerned only with foods and drinks, various washing, and fleshly ordinances imposed until the time of reformation. But Christ came as High Priest of the good things to come, with the greater and more perfect tabernacle not made with hands, that is, not of this*

*creation. Not with the blood of goats and calves, but with His own blood He entered the Most Holy Place once for all, having obtained eternal redemption. For if the blood of bulls and goats and the ashes of a heifer, sprinkling the unclean, sanctifies for the purifying of the flesh, how much more shall the blood of Christ, who through the eternal Spirit offered Himself without spot to God, cleanse your conscience from dead works to serve the living God?"* (Heb 9:9-14).

The sacrifices under the old covenant could not make man perfect in regard to conscience, it continually made him who offered sacrifice conscious of sins and had to be repeated year after year. Christ entered the Most Holy place by His own blood, not the blood of cows and goats which could not remove sins. *"There is no forgiveness of sins without the shedding of blood"* (Heb 9:22). **The only commodity which could remove sin was blood, no amount of dialogue or self pity the victim could utter before God could earn them forgiveness.** No amount of confession can make God forgive us, forgiveness required blood. We can't substitute the blood of Jesus with anything else.

Christ obtained an eternal redemption for mankind, not temporary redemption which can be challenged by our behavior or circumstances but eternal. He offered Himself through the eternal Spirit and the results have eternal consequences, they far much outweigh the failure in Adam which was temporary and have been reversed by the blood of Jesus. God transcends time, He lives above time. He is not subject to time, today, tomorrow or yesterday. Whatever He does has eternal consequences. The sacrifice He offered had eternal significance, the word He speaks resonates eternally. Man stands redeemed through the blood of Jesus *"Not with the blood of goats and calves, but with His own blood He entered the Most Holy Place once for all, having obtained eternal redemption."* (Heb 9:12). Unfortunately we have taken the blood of Jesus in the same level as the blood of cows and goats which could temporarily cover sins and never removed sin. Christ's blood has once for all dealt with sin eternally. His blood secured our total forgiveness and redemption from all sins and His resurrection ensured we are not guilty of any sin, no sin will ever be charged against you. The lamb of God took the sins of the whole world. It is a mockery to the power of the blood of Jesus to continually ask God to forgive us our sins, we make the blood of Jesus of the same level as the blood of cows and goats which only covered sins and required to be continually offered. It was just a temporary covering for sins, but now we have been clothed with Christ the perfect garment that has removed every trace of sin. One sacrifice was enough to deal with all our past, present and future sins. *"We have redemption through His blood the forgiveness of sins,"* (Eph 1:7). Sin was the hindering factor, God bought us back by forgiving us our sins thus securing our eternal redemption.

## Judgment Satisfied
*"For Christ has not entered the holy places made with hands, which are copies of the true, but into heaven itself, now to appear in the presence of God for us; not that He should offer Himself often, as the high priest enters the Most Holy Place every year*

*with blood of another— He then would have had to suffer often since the foundation of the world; but now, once at the end of the ages, He has appeared to put away sin by the sacrifice of Himself."* (Heb 9:24-26)

He entered the Holy of Holies in heavens itself to appear before the presence of God for us. He was the perfect intercessor who stood before God with His blood for us thus putting away sin by the sacrifice of Himself. He totally satisfied the judgment on sin. In God's mind sin has conclusively been dealt with forever. *"And if Christ has not risen, your faith is a vain thing — you are still in your sins. His resurrection is evidence your sins are forgiven."* (1 Cor 15:17, WEY)

*"And as it is appointed for men to die once, but after this the judgment, so Christ was offered once to bear the sins of many. To those who eagerly wait for Him He will appear a second time, apart from sin, for salvation."* (Heb 9:27-28). It was appointed for Christ to die once and face judgment for sin. He satisfied judgment for sin, so Christ was once offered to bear the sins of many and shall appear a second time not to deal with sins but to save those who wait for His appearance. *"The same goes for everyone: man dies only once, and then faces judgment. Christ died once, and faced the judgment of the entire human race! His second appearance has nothing to do with sin, but to reveal salvation for all to lay a hold of Him."* (Heb 9:27-28, Mirror)

This means no other sacrifice for sin will ever be offered since God was satisfied with the sacrifice offered. And because God was satisfied, there is no more judgement on account of sin. It is not legal to judge one crime twice, once somebody has been convicted for a crime and has been sentenced and served the sentence it is not legal to accuse him for the same crime again. Christ suffered on account of our sins and faced judgement for the same, therefore God will not judge us again for the same crime. In the Old Testament wherever there was sin in the camp among the people and a plague broke out, when a sacrifice was offered the plague stopped, why because the sacrificial lamb bore the guilt of the sinner and the plague stopped. We should not live with fear of judgment, the lamb of God took our guilt and sin and was punished on our behalf. *"Much more, then, having been declared righteous now in his blood, we shall be saved through him from the wrath; for if, being enemies, we have been reconciled to God through the death of His Son, much more, having been reconciled, we shall be saved in his life."* (Romans 5:9-10, YLT).

*"By that will we have been sanctified through the offering of the* **body of Jesus Christ once for all.** *And every priest stands ministering daily and offering repeatedly the same sacrifices, which can never take away sins.* **But this Man, after He had offered one sacrifice for sins forever, sat down at the right hand of God,** *"* ( Heb 10:10-12).

Through the sacrifice of the body of Christ once for all time we have been sanctified. One sacrifice for sin took care of sin forever. The writer has severally repeated the fact that the sacrifices under the old system could not take away sins. The purpose is to distinguish the former from the new which was

121

offered once and accomplished an eternal purpose of removing sin. **The fact that He sat down communicates to us that the work of atonement was completely finished.** The priests under the former covenant never had the privilege of sitting in the temple or the tent of meeting. The tabernacle was not furnished with chairs, because their work was never to be finished. They had to work day after day covering sins. The blood of cows and bulls could not remove sin, it always served as a reminder of sin every time the sacrifices were offered. (Heb. 10:1-4). The blood of Christ dealt with sin once for all. The fact that He does not die daily means forgiveness is not granted on daily basis, it was offered once. By one sacrifice he has conclusively dealt with sin and our sanctification, it is upon us to realize this and walk in what God has already finished. *"And you know that He was manifested to take away our sins, and in Him there is no sin."* (1 John 3:5)

*"Therefore, when he come into the world, He said, Sacrifice and offering you did not desire, but a body you have prepared me:"* (Heb 10:5). The priests under the old system could only offer animal sacrifices for sin which were far much of less value than the human life itself. Christ did not offer an animal sacrifice but His own body as a sacrifice which represented the complete value of man made in God's image. The value of the sacrifice speaks volumes to us. It accomplished the desired results. **If you wish to know the value of the blood of Jesus look at what it redeemed.**

### Holy Spirit Witnesses

The Holy Spirit bears witness about our sins being forgiven, *"For by one offering He has perfected forever those who are being sanctified. But the Holy Spirit also witnesses to us; for after He had said before, "This is the covenant that I will make with them after those days, says the LORD: I will put My laws into their hearts, and in their minds I will write them," {#Jer 31:33}then He adds, "Their sins and their lawless deeds I will remember no more." {#Jer 31:34}"* (Heb 10:15-17). The Holy Spirit bears witness that there is no more remembrance of sins because they have been forgiven. Love never keeps a record of wrongs, our loving God will never keep records of wrongs we have done. Now if God does not remember your sins, has forgiven your sins and has thrown them to the pit of forgetfulness, who then will judge you for the same? God declares *"I, even I, am He who blots out your transgressions for My own sake; And I will not remember your sins."* (Isa 43:25).

You have no reason to walk with sin consciousness, the blood has taken care of all our past, present and future sins. In the mind of God there is no more sacrifice which will ever be offered to deal with sin again, it has already been dealt with. **When Christ died on the cross all our sins were in the future,** we were yet to sin, apart from what Adam did. None of us living today was born by then yet Christ died for our sins. Did His blood only take care of the sins we have committed? Does He have to die again every time we fall into sin? The conclusion is clear; all our sins past, present and future were taken care of by one sacrifice.

That's why God Has never called you a sinner, He understands the complete work of the cross. God is not apologetic living in us, He dealt with sin with full knowledge of our future life. If God has declared us forgiven, no one should bring any charge against us. This does not give us a license to walk in sin, the seed of God in us will not manifest sin but the life of God. Any person who fully believes this will forever be grateful to God for lifting this burden of sin from their lives and they will manifest the character which God has intended for us.

*"And when sins have been forgiven, there is no need to offer any more sacrifices. "* (Heb.10:18, New Living Translation).

Because sins have been dealt with, there is no more sacrifice to be offered day after day and Jesus doesn't have to suffer every year for our sins. We have received eternal forgiveness, walk with a clean conscience regarding your sins. The sins were dealt with at the cross of Christ, the cross was not a failure but a success. We don't need to behave like the people who lived before the cross, they depended on the blood of cows which could not remove sins. Their sins were covered on credit but the blood of Jesus removed sin completely from the mind of God. **If it's not in God's mind then it does not exist.**

Could this be the one thing you have struggled with for long? Could this be the news which will forever set you free from condemnation to sin? You are free and sin no longer has dominance over your life, it was completely rubbed off from God's mind. *"This is final: I have deleted the record of your sins and misdeeds. I no longer recall them. (Nothing in God's reference of man, reminds Him of sin.) Sins were dealt with in such a thorough manner that no further offerings would ever be required. Nothing we can personally sacrifice could add further virtue to our innocence."* (Heb 10: 17-18 Mirror) This was the message Paul preached to people in his day. *"Therefore let it be known to you, brethren, that through this Man is preached to you the forgiveness of sins;"* (Acts 13:38). Under the old system, when a sinner brought a sacrifice for sin, the priest could examine the animal to see if it was blameless. The purpose for doing this was to ensure the sinner took the blameless and perfect life of the animal and the animal died with the sin of the sinner. The sin was dead. **At no moment did the priest examine the sinner before or after the sacrifice**. An exchange took place, the man walked away with the blameless and perfect life of the animal. Christ the lamb of God was examined by the Jewish high priest and found without a fault, He was blameless, He took our sins and died with them. We have taken His blameless and perfect life. There is no more examination left for us, the sin life died with the lamb.

Paul speaks something to us *"Examine yourselves as to whether you are in the faith. Test yourselves. Do you not know yourselves, that Jesus Christ is in you? —unless indeed you are disqualified."* (2 Cor 13:5). Examine yourself to see if Christ is in you. This is the examination you need, if He is in you it is enough. You need nothing more, you have taken His blameless life and in God's mind you are blameless. *"Just as He chose us in Him before the foundation of the world, that we should be holy and without blame before Him in love,"* (Eph 1:4). It's not in heaven that we shall be blameless as we have been taught, but here in this life. We are blameless before Him and it was predestined to be so.

## 1 John

1 John has been one of the most controversial scriptures which address the issue of forgiveness of sins. It has greatly been misinterpreted to mean what the writer never had in mind when he wrote it. It has also been addressed to the wrong people who the writer did not address it to. As we read scriptures we should be aware of why a specific scripture was written, to whom it was addressed, who the writer had in mind, what was he addressing?

*"If we say that we have no sin, we deceive ourselves, and the truth is not in us. If we confess our sins, He is faithful and just to forgive us our sins and to cleanse us from all unrighteousness. If we say that we have not sinned, we make Him a liar, and His word is not in us."* (1 John 1:8-10).

"If we say we have no sin, we deceive ourselves." Does the Bible contradict itself by telling us we have been forgiven yet we have to still admit we are sinners? The only way to solve this puzzle is to know who is John addressing in these verses. He has just told us in verse 7 *"if we walk in the light as He is in the light, we have fellowship with one another, and the blood of Jesus Christ His Son cleanses us from all sin."* The blood takes care of our sins as children of the light. We don't get out of the light when we sin and then restored after cleansing, while we are in the light and have fellowship with him the blood secures and ensures the fellowship continues.

How possible could the blood of Jesus cleanse us from all sin and yet still be sinners? John again tells us *"People conceived and brought into life by God don't make a practice of sin. How could they? God's seed is deep within them, making them who they are. It's not in the nature of the God-begotten to practice and parade sin. "* (1 John 3:9, Message) People who have been born of God who don't have a practice of sinning how could he call them sinners? Definitely he must be speaking about another group not us who walk in the light and are the sons of God and who the blood cleanses.

John was addressing an erratic group called the Gnostics who had risen several years after the church was born. The Gnostics had denied Jesus came in the flesh, they taught that Jesus could not have walked this planet on a physical body because the body is evil and the spiritual is divine. John addresses this teaching at the beginning of this letter in chapter one by affirming he was with Christ physically. They heard Him, they saw Him and they touched Him, he goes on to say *"Beloved, do not believe every spirit, but test the spirits, whether they are of God; because many false prophets have gone out into the world. By this you know the Spirit of God: Every spirit that confesses that Jesus Christ has come in the flesh is of God, and every spirit that does not confess that Jesus Christ has come in the flesh is not of God. And this is the spirit of the Antichrist, which you have heard was coming, and is now already in the world. "* ( 1 John 4:1-3).

The Gnostics also denied the reality of sin, they taught sin was not real because it took place in the physical realm and therefore it could not affect our spiritual life. They taught you could do anything in the physical, live the way you want because after all this will not be part of you, it is just in the physical. John addresses this teaching in verse 8, *"if we say we have no sin we deceive ourselves, if we say we have not sinned we make God a liar* (and Christ died for nothing). *'But if we confess,* (we agree with God on the reality of sin) *then God is faithful and just to forgive us our sins and to cleanse us from all unrighteousness."* There are many today who behave like the Gnostics who have not accepted the reality of the cross of Christ and its full effect on the life of man. To deny sin existed is to deny the event of the cross ever took place. Sin existed that's why Christ faced the cross to deal with it. The unbeliever still walks in the sin of unbelief.

**The fact that He cleanses us from all unrighteousness means once you have been cleansed there is no more cleansing to be done**. All means all; therefore we can not continue with a lifestyle of mentioning sins everyday. It is the unbeliever who agrees with God on the existence of sin especially unbelief in Christ and the fact that Jesus died for sins. He agrees with God on the reality of the cross, and accepts this forgiveness in his life, not the believer who already believes and has been cleansed. But we make a practice of preaching to believers asking them to admit they are sinners every day. Once they admit they are sinners everyday, when will they enjoy the forgiveness of sins? When will they enjoy righteousness in Christ? The devil will always remind them they are sinners and the cycle of confessing sins continues day after day.

The fact that he uses the word 'us' does not mean that he is addressing believers. He has also used the words 'we' in verse 8 and 10. What John is implying here is we humans say there is no sin, If we agree with God and change our minds (repent), He cleanses us from all our unrighteousness. He has severally addressed believers as beloved, my little children.

## Advocate

In addressing believers John writes *"My little children, these things I write to you, so that you may not sin. And if anyone sins, we have an Advocate with the Father, Jesus Christ the righteous. And He Himself is the propitiation for our sins, and not for ours only but also for the whole world."* (1 John 2:1-2).

God understood that we are not immune to sinning, we are not suppose to sin but if we happen to sin we have an advocate who stands before the Father on our behalf, He is the atoning sacrifice for our sins and not just ours but the sins of the whole world. You can approach God asking Him to forgive you, but unfortunately that's all you can do, you have nothing to present before the Judge, you do not understand the court language. You don't need to do all that, you are represented. **The advocate Jesus Christ understands the court language and has a much stronger evidence to present against sin, His blood.** His blood testifies against your sins, that's what the judge wants to hear, not your list of wrongs you have done. He is the one who stands before the judge and tells Him of the sins of the whole world, what His blood has accomplished for the sins of the whole world.

Again John writes *"I write to you, little children, because your sins are forgiven you for His name's sake."* (1 John 2:12).

Imagine the issue of forgiveness of sins to John is not an issue of the fathers but of children still young in faith who need to be assured of their sins forgiven, it is an elementary teaching. Fathers are dealing with issues beyond forgiveness of sins. Our sins are already forgiven. The epistles address the forgiveness of sins as a past event not a future event. It has already happened, you need not waste your energy begging for forgiveness, it is not your responsibility, there is an advocate whom God has appointed for us, and it is His responsibility to address the issue of your sin. This is part of what we have received from God freely and the Holy Spirit came to reveal to us.

Suppose this testament was based on you asking always to be forgiven, then it could have failed long time ago. What if you forget to ask for forgiveness? What if you sin unconsciously, what about the evil thoughts that cross our minds? Does the testament fail? God promised *"their sins and iniquity I will remember no more."* That promise was never given with a condition. We always quote 2 Chro 7:14, One man who was God Himself, humbled and took our form, and died the death of a criminal, He interceded for us and His sacrifice was accepted. God heard us through Him, forgave our sins and healed our land. Heb 8:8-13 overrides it. Christ is the guarantor of this testament not you. *"And you know that He was manifested to take away our sins, and in Him there is no sin."* (1 John 3:5)

If you believe your forgiveness is dependent on your confession, then it means to the degree you confess (you ask for forgiveness of your sins) to God to the same degree you will be forgiven. It means if you fail to mention all your sins always then you will only be forgiven to the level you have asked. Look at God's generosity (Matt 9:2-8), the man sick of palsy did not ask Christ for forgiveness of sins, but before healing him He forgave him unconditionally without the man requesting.

## Confession.

What does this word confession mean? It has greatly been used in our Christian circles to mean something else than what the writers had in mind. Confession today has been used to imply taking a list of our sins and failures to God and asking Him to forgive us. The word 'confess' comes from the Greek word "*homologeo*" It means to say the same thing as another, to agree with. When the writer says we confess he simply means we say the same thing God says, we agree with God. It is not only about our sins that we agree with God but in all aspects of life we should agree with what God says about us.

We should confess what God says about our lives, our health, our finances, our families, our entire being. Definitely God is not saying that we are sinners after the event of the cross. You have no basis giving Him a list of your sins, He calls you the righteousness of God in Christ Jesus. God's testimony is greater than man's testimony. Whose testimony will you believe? If you happen to sin, the advocate takes care of the situation. In this testament, He promises never to remember our sins, it's not when we confess but the testament states clearly there is no sin to be remembered. There is no record to be kept about our sin, no angel up there recording our wrongs, but religion will always remind us of our sins, and the moment we keep asking for forgiveness we feel we have played a part to earn forgiveness of sins. Forgiveness was granted unconditionally.

If you are doing something wrong and you know this is contrary to what God says about us, you have one obligation, admit to yourself this is not true of my new nature and is not right for me to continue this way, agree with what God says, this is wrong of you and thank God for the forgiveness of sins, confess you are forgiven. Our conscience will always awaken us to know the way to go and when we miss that way. God has chiseled His desire in our conscience, He says, *"...I will put my laws in their mind and write them on their hearts; and I will be their God and they shall be my people."* (Heb 8:10). When you know this is not the way, turn from the wrong thing to what you know God agrees with. Even if you tell God you are sorry already you know the blood took care of the situation. Telling God only addresses our minds not God, it does not change anything. Confession should remind us of our forgiven status, it does not buy us forgiveness. True repentance is a change of mind.

What believers do is to repent, the word repent comes from a Greek word *"metanoeo,"* it means to change ones mind. When we realize we are not walking in the right path, we change our minds and get to the right track. Its like the pianist playing a note on his piano, at the back of his mind he knows how the tune should sound, should he make a mistake and hit a wrong button, he quickly changes and hits the right button and gets what he had anticipated in his mind.

Our conscience is our teacher, it always alert us when we are going on the wrong. We have borrowed much from the dark ages where the church sold penance or indulgences to people to get forgiveness. People could go to great lengths tormenting their bodies to earn forgiveness. The same word penance has been translated to mean repent, to ask God for forgiveness. **True repentance occurs when we change our minds to what God says about us.** Confess what God says about you, you are righteous, yes and ought not to sin. Sin is contrary to what God knows and says about you, change to what you know is right according to the new nature you have received.

The early church never knew how to ask God for forgiveness of sin, no Pauline epistle mentions we ask God for forgiveness of sins. If it is a requirement, then all the churches Paul ministered to never heard that revelation. Paul speaks in his writings about baptism, holy communion, prayer, giving, fellowship, praising God, marriage, church government and more others. If confession of sin was very important, why could he not mention it even once? All the churches Peter ministered to lacked that knowledge, yet today we seem to have that knowledge. Where did we get this?

James also speaks about confession, (James 5:16), he says we should confess our sin one to another. What he simply means, if I wrong you and you are my brother, the noble thing to do is to approach you and settle the issue and come into agreement. We should settle our disagreement one to another and agree to walk together admitting when we have wronged another. We also should share our struggles one with another, in doing this you will find help from your fellow believer. When we share our challenges one to another we are able to help each other. When we sin, we sin only against God, the only thing that atones for sin is blood. We may offend our brothers or do wrong against them, we ought to apologize to them and reconcile with them. Should we be sinning against our brothers then we would need blood sacrifice to atone for our sin always. As our new nature requires we live at peace with all men, we should have the courtesy of approaching our fellow men when we offend them and agree with them what ought to be right. Confess one to another and make peace and share our challenges and help each other.

## Convict

What about the Holy Spirit convicting us of our sins? This is another deception the enemy has sold to us. We have believed the Holy Spirit is in business of assessing our behavior and whenever we do wrong He will not let us off the hook. He will put guilt in our hearts until we confess (mention the sin) to God. You may be very sincere in your confession, sincerity does not qualify truth. You may be sincere but sincerely wrong. **There is no where in the epistle where the Holy Spirit convicts believers of sin.** The word convict is a judicial term which means "to find guilty." Once someone has been found guilty and sentenced to jail we call him a convict. Does the Holy Spirit find us guilty? Guilty of what? He bears witness that there is no more remembrance of sin. The only place where the Holy Spirit is mentioned to convict is in John 16:8.

*"Nevertheless I tell you the truth. It is to your advantage that I go away; for if I do not go away, the Helper will not come to you; but if I depart, I will send Him to you. "And when He has come, He will convict the world of sin, and of righteousness, and of judgment: "of sin, because they do not believe in me; "of righteousness, because I go to My Father and you see me no more; "of judgment, because the ruler of this world is judged."* (Vs 7-11).

The Holy Spirit convicts the world of sin because they do not believe in Him. He does not convict believers of sin, we are not of the world, we have been separated from the world. He convicts us of righteousness. He tells the disciples, *"I go to the father and "you" see me no more. "* He was addressing "you" the disciple and not the world. He tells us how righteous we have become in Christ, He has gone to the Father and we see Him no more yet the Spirit will convict us of righteousness because we share in His righteousness. We are guilty of righteousness not of sin and the Holy Spirit always points this to us.

I visited a town for evangelistic meetings one time, we were given accommodation in one of the pastors house. A fellow pastor who had invited us to the town gave me some negative story about this pastor who was hosting us and he wanted me to confront this pastor and ask him about these incidences he was telling me. I never wanted to get into what I was not part of so I stuck to my agenda of winning souls. On the last night of the meeting as I was praying for people, the Holy Spirit gave me a word for this pastor who was being accused. To my surprise God never spoke anything negative about him, it surprised all the pastors who were there. This man went down in tears when he received the word how God loved him and approved him. It taught me a lesson, God will always speak well of us, that's what He knows of us.

The enemy takes advantage of our ignorance of this truth and whenever we sin he fills our minds with condemnation and often we believe it is the Holy Spirit convicting us. Sometime we take time to pray and fast to remove the guilt thinking it is from God. God has no business reminding you of your sins, once forgiven always forgiven. John says *"if our heart condemns us, God is greater than our heart, and knows all things."* (1 John 3:20). When you feel guilt and condemnation in your heart run to what God says and knows about you. God is greater than your heart. His testimony carries more authority than what you feel in your heart. It is natural to feel sorry when you have done wrong because it is contrary to who you are, Godly sorrow is not condemning, it does not lead us into guilt. Godly sorrow leads us to repentance, change of mind.

**God has no business filling us with condemnation.** Paul declares to us after pointing out his struggles with the sin of covetousness, the guilt and condemnation that always followed him in Romans 7 by telling us, *"There is therefore now no condemnation for those who are in Christ Jesus."* (Romans 8:1, RSV). Other translations have additions which were not in the original writings. The translators could not imagine unconditional no condemnation, they added a condition. God clearly says there is now no condemnation to whoever is in

Christ. The time you feel you are on the wrong, that is the now moment and God says He does not condemn you. Christ did not condemn the woman caught in adultery, the first thing He did was to remove the condemnation. When people feel they are not condemned they will walk free, but once they feel condemned they are led away from God and feel vulnerable to continue in sin. Prisoners who serve their sentence in jail upon release they come home, if the community does not accept them but still condemns them, they will always find their way back to crime and back to jail. In jail their colleagues do not condemn them. God has removed the condemnation from us, now He says sin no more. God will never condemn you, He condemned sin on Christ on your behalf and for all your sins.

The Holy Spirit convicts unbelievers not of sins but of sin (singular). The sin which the unbeliever is guilty of is unbelief. Unbelief is what will hinder many from enjoying eternal life with God. Just as it was in the wilderness, they committed all kinds of evil but what is mentioned is unbelief (Heb 3:19). They failed to enter the land of promise because of unbelief. The blood of the lamb had secured their release from bondage to Pharaoh, all Jews were set free from Egypt, but unbelief kept them from the promised land. The wilderness was a product of unbelief. They saw all miracles you can imagine of but still perished in the wilderness because of unbelief. The supernatural is not the evidence of faith.

Jesus promised a day will come when all sin men have committed will be forgiven. *"Therefore I say to you, every sin and blasphemy will be forgiven men, but the blasphemy against the Spirit will not be forgiven men."* (Matt 12:31). The word every in Greek is "pas pas," it implies both individual and collective, it means 'every' and 'all.' He promised when all sin will be forgiven men. The cross took care of all sin. Only blasphemy against the Spirit, "unbelief" will not be taken care of. There is no remedy against unbelief. It is the Spirit of God who ministers salvation to us, if we fail to believe Him how can we be saved?

*"Seventy weeks are determined on your people and on your holy city, to finish the transgression, and to make an end of sins, and to make reconciliation for iniquity, and to bring in everlasting righteousness, and to seal up the vision and prophecy, and to anoint the most Holy."* (Dan 9:24). All these were to be accomplished by the coming of the messiah, He dealt with sin and made reconciliation for iniquity. He also brought everlasting righteousness, that's His own righteousness.

On the Day of Atonement all Jews were included in the sacrifice which the high priest offered on behalf of the entire nation. When he came out of the Holy of Hollies, every Jew believed their sins were atoned for. There was jubilation in the nation, God had received the offering for sin and their sins had completely been atoned for. They knew blessings will follow them for a whole year not curses. So did Christ our high priest, He entered the Holy of Hollies on our behalf with His own blood and obtained an eternal redemption for our sins. **When He rose from the grave it was clear that the sacrifice had been received and our sins had**

**been atoned for,** we now live expecting blessings not curses. We have to believe on His finished work and know the years ahead will be full of blessings for us.

Does this put an urge in your heart to sin or do you feel relieved you don't have to carry a burden for your sins always? I'm sure you feel relieved, I'm sure it has not given you a license to walk in sin but freedom to live the life of God. Sin is contrary to our nature. When you are vaccinated against typhoid and your body is resistant to typhoid causing bacteria, does this give you a license to go everywhere drinking sewer water? Will you forget the need to maintain high hygienic standards? Should you do that, you risk getting other infections which your body may not be able to resist. God has dealt with sin and removed the condemnation in our lives that we may sin no more. We have not received the Spirit of sin but of righteousness. We have received a new heart of flesh not of stone. Any believer who walks in sin is still under the law and not under grace. It is the law that empowers sin in our lives (1 Cor 15:56), grace overcomes sin in our lives.

**The Communion Table.**
What about at the communion table, should we examine and see if we have sins in our lives before taking the communion? (1 Cor 11:23-34). Whoever eats the bread and drinks the cup should discern that it was this cup and this bread that took our judgment for sin, when we fail to discern this, we keep ourselves under condemnation because we fail to realize the judgment was passed on His body for us. Many are sick and dead because they failed to discern their healing in this cup and bread, they took the

cup and the bread but did not see their healing paid for in the sacrifice.

*"To see oneself associated in Christ's death and declared innocent in His blood is the only worthy manner in which to examine one's own life in the context of the New Testament meal. Anyone who partakes this meal in an indifferent manner, either because of religious sentiment or merely being blasé about the meaning of the meal, eats and drinks judgment upon himself! The human body of Jesus represents judgment of every human life: to fail to realize this is to deliberately exclude your self from the blessing of the new covenant."*

*"This is the reason why many of you are suffering with weaknesses and illnesses, and many have already died. By judging that we indeed co-died in His death we are free from any kind of judgment! By discerning the broken body of Christ we can only conclude that He was wounded for our transgression and that indeed the chastisement that brought us peace was upon Him; this is the instruction of the Lord; What foolishness it will be to continue to place yourself and the rest of the world under judgment when Jesus already took all judgment upon Himself."* (1 Cor 11:28-32, Mirror Bible). (John 5:22) **All judgment was given to the son, what did He do with the judgment? He took it upon Himself on the cross.**

God has no business judging you. Discern your freedom and healing in the cup and body of Christ. When we take the communion with this understanding we will experience miracles in our communion services. The communion is not the table for our sins, it's about Jesus Christ, it's the Lord's table, it's for His remembrance not remembrance of your sins. We have turned it to a platform to remember every sin we did. The Lord's table is an opportunity to bring forward the experience which happened 2000 years ago to the present day. We experience what happened as if it is happening today and participate in its benefits, it's an opportunity to remember the cross.

The communion also speaks to us of incarnation. When we partake of our meals, the meal is absorbed and becomes part of our body, we can not separate the meal from the body. In the incarnation God become one with us without a separation, we celebrate this union in our meals. It is through eating that sin entered and death through sin, also through eating the communion we partake of His life and healing in our bodies.

### God's Goodness

What a joy to know that all my sins were completely dealt with and there is no day I will be judged on regard to sin. I am eternally secure and have no reason to worry about walking out of fellowship with God. No scripture in the epistles supports the idea of walking out of and walking into fellowship with God when we sin. Heb 13:5 declares "He will never leave you nor forsake you," unconditionally, we are eternally united. My fellowship with Him is not dependant on my sin. Sin can not overcome God's grace in my life, God's grace overcomes sin in my life, neither can it scare Him away, remember He became sin itself. This gives me every reason to walk with thanks giving always in my heart. We all have been forgiven much therefore we should appreciate much.

**It is not repentance that leads us to see God's goodness. God's goodness leads men to repentance.** (Rom 2:4). When we see all the good God has done for us, we have no reason to harden our hearts but we change our minds. Our hearts have been designed to respond to love. We have been designed to respond to good news. When my team scores, no one teaches me ten steps to begin cheering, it is automatic I will jump up and shout. When your spirit hears good news, it knows how to respond. Listen to what this Old Testament prophet knew about God even before the cross of Christ, *"Where is another God like you, who pardons the guilt of the remnant, overlooking the sins of his special people? You will not stay angry with your people forever, because you delight in showing unfailing love. Once again you will have compassion on us. You will trample our sins under your feet and throw them into the depths of the ocean!"* (Micah 7:18-19, NLT). And the good news is that it has happened through the cross of Christ. *"Love prospers when a fault is forgiven, but dwelling on it separates close friends."* (Prov 17:9, NLT)

The psalmist discovered a secret which we need to know, *"Out of the depths I have cried to You, O LORD; Lord, hear my voice! Let Your ears be attentive To the voice of my supplications. If You, LORD, should mark iniquities, O Lord, who could stand? But there is forgiveness with You, That You may be feared."* (Ps 130:1-4). **God is not feared because He punishes sin but**

**because He forgives sins**. Forgiving is the nature of our God, He does not keep a record of wrongs. Love keeps no record of wrongs. If He kept, none of us could survive. Unfortunately we keep a record of wrongs that's why we are held in the tradition of mentioning our sins every day. Listen to this translation *"If you, GOD, kept records on wrongdoings, who would stand a chance? As it turns out, forgiveness is your habit, and that's why you're worshiped."* (Message) That's why He forgave the sick man of His sins without him asking (Matt. 9:2-8). It's God's goodness that leads us to repentance, (Rom 2:4). God's desire is to overwhelm you with His goodness until you can't resist changing your mind. He makes His sun to shine on the godly and ungodly and makes His rain to shower on both the godly and the ungodly.

*"Blessed is he whose transgression is forgiven, Whose sin is covered. Blessed is the man to whom the LORD does not impute iniquity, And in whose spirit there is no deceit."* (Ps 32:1-2). David writes about this blessed person whose transgression is forgiven, and his sin is covered, and God does not impute iniquity on him. We all know David suffered the consequence for his sin of murder and counting the fighting men. So he is not referring to himself but he saw it coming to us. God has forgiven us completely and not only covered our sins but removed them by the cross of Jesus Christ and does not impute sin on us any more. This is God's wisdom, how God see things with a clear vision, we speak this wisdom among the mature as Paul says. If God should punish us for sin then He will apologize to Jesus who bore the wrath for our sins and has become one with us.

# SEVEN

## NEWNESS OF LIFE

Dear beloved, I know after such an exposition many are struggling with this thought, shall we continue in sin? Are we trying to make light of the sin issue and giving people a license to walk in sin? Is this what the Word of God teaches? On the contrary, personally I Bonface don't promote sin neither do I entertain sin.

After Paul's writing in Romans 5 about the contrast between Adam and Christ, he concludes Romans 5 by writing in Vs 20-21 *"All that passing laws against sin did was produce more lawbreakers. But sin didn't, and doesn't, have a chance in competition with the **aggressive forgiveness we call grace. When it's sin versus grace, grace wins hands down.** All sin can do is threaten us with death, and that's the end of it. Grace, because God is putting everything together again through the Messiah, invites us into life—a life that goes on and on and on, world without end."* (Message, )

Should Paul be alive today I believe he could be a stranger in many pulpits, how could he say grace wins hands down and yet sin carries the day in our preaching every week? Paul felt in his mind the legalists could accuse him of giving people a license to walk in sin. He begins Romans 6 by addressing the issue of sin.

*"So what do we do? Keep on sinning so God can keep on forgiving? I should hope not! If we've left the country where sin is sovereign, how can we still live in our old house there? Or didn't you realize **we packed up and left there for good?** That is what happened in baptism. When we went under the water, we left **the old country of sin behind;** when we came up out of the water, we entered into the new country of grace—a new life in a new land! That's what baptism into the life of Jesus means. When we are lowered into the water, it is like the burial of Jesus; when we are raised up out of the water, it is like the resurrection of Jesus."* (Rom. 6:1-4, Message).

We died to sin through the body of Christ and we cannot continue in it. How can we be dead to sin and alive to sin at the same time? We packed and left that house for good, trying to live in sin is going back to the former house which we left for good. God transferred us through the death of Christ on the cross and baptism pictures what happened to us.

Paul brings us to the reality of what has happened to us. We shared in the death of Christ and we were raised with him. *"Certainly not! How shall we who died to sin live any longer in it? Or do you not know that as many of us as were baptized into Christ Jesus were baptized into His death?"* ( Vs 2-3). We died to sin, the wages of sin is death, when sin reigned in our bodies it led to the death on the cross. Sin killed us on the cross and we were raised to another life, another world where sin is not sovereign.

We left that country where sin ruled and we came to another country where we enjoy resurrection life apart from sin. Sin did not die but we died and left that country of sin. The body which sin used to rule and dominate was killed and died and therefore sin could not rule in a dead body. God raised us from the dead not in the sin dominated life but to another life, another country. He crucified the body of sin. Imagine joining a military training school, you get a trainer who is so harsh and often harasses you wherever he meets you in the camp. Anytime he meets you, he asks you to do fifty push-ups, run twenty times round the field. You get tired of his harassments and you resign from the training. Next time you are in the streets you meet this former instructor and he orders you to do fifty push-ups, will you obey him again? That's what happened between you and sin.

**Knowledge**
Knowledge is vital, *"knowing this, that our old man was crucified with Him, that the body of sin might be done away with, that we should no longer be slaves of sin."* (Rom. 6:6). The vehicle that accommodated sin in us was scrapped and rendered entirely useless. Without being cognisant of this we shall still yield ourselves to sin and yet we were relocated to another country. He uses the Greek word "*ginosko*" which means "to learn to know, to get knowledge of, to perceive."

We need to get this knowledge that our old man was crucified with Him. With this knowledge being part of us we can not continue in sin. Sin illegally operates through us, its operating system was crucified on the cross, being cognisant of this we can not give sin a leeway in our lives. *"He who has died has been freed from the power of sin."*(Vs 7). *"If nothing stops you from doing something wrong, death certainly does."* (Mirror) We are not alive to sin, we died with Christ. The fact that death took place means we owe sin nothing. We are not indebted to fulfill its lusts and desires.

*"Knowing that Christ, having been raised from the dead, dies no more. Death no longer has dominion over Him."* (Rom. 6:9). He uses another different Greek word for knowing *"eido"* which means to "see, to perceive with the eyes and the senses." He is bringing out something practical to us. We don't need just to educate our minds but to see ourselves in the death of Christ to sin. Our senses should perceive this, anytime we see or touch that which is evil our senses should be aroused to the fact that we died with Christ and death as a result of sin has no more dominion. Having this knowledge and perceiving with our senses that death has taken place which we were part of. We should attend our funeral in our minds, it took place 2000 years ago. When our senses comprehend this, we won't have any reason to submit to sinful desires. Death as a result of sin will not put us down again. It's not something we guess but we see, it happened. *"When Jesus died, he took sin down with him, but alive he brings God down to us."* (Vs 10, Message). His life now exhibits our union with the life of God.

*"Likewise you also, reckon yourselves to be dead indeed to sin, but alive to God in Christ Jesus our Lord. Therefore do not let sin*

*reign in your mortal body, that you should obey it in its lusts."*
(Rom. 6:11-12 )

Paul here uses another different word for reckon, he uses the Greek word "*logizomai*" which means to "count, to calculate, compute, come to logical conclusion,'' it is not a supposition but a fact. It's a fact which every believer should have in mind, come to logical conclusion that we are indeed dead to sin and alive to God. Even when we have some negative feelings in our body, it should not change the fact that we died to sin. Many believers have given up on what Paul says about our death to sin because of the desires we feel rising from our body, and we try to die to sin daily. **There is nothing like dying to sin daily, count it as a fact that we are already dead to sin.** *"This reasoning is equally relevant to you. Calculate the cross; there can only be one logical conclusion: He died your death; that means you died unto sin, and are now alive unto God. Sin-consciousness can never again feature in your future! You are in Christ Jesus; His Lordship is the authority of this union."* (Rom 6:11, Mirror). Do not allow sin to reign, to govern and to have lordship over you. Make this logical conclusion about sin. Sin consciousness can not be part of you. Don't see yourself a sinner but a saint.

*"And do not present your members as instruments of unrighteousness to sin, but present yourselves to God as being alive from the dead, and your members as instruments of righteousness to God. For sin shall not have dominion over you, for you are not under law but under grace."* (Rom. 6:13).

Paul tells us not to present our members, the word present is a Greek word "*paristemi*" which means to "place beside or near" We should not let our members loose in the vicinity of unrighteousness where sin can seize and use them. Rather we place our members in readiness to God as weapons of righteousness. When sin knocks in our minds with thoughts of lust, we should not entertain those thoughts, we should not allow sin to seize our thoughts and lead us into unrighteousness but should yield our thoughts to God to be used as instruments of righteousness.

*"Sin can't tell you how to live. After all, you're not living under that old tyranny any longer. You're living in the freedom of God. So, since we're out from under the old tyranny, does that mean we can live any old way we want? Since we're free in the freedom of God, can we do anything that comes to mind?"* (Rom 6:14-15, Message). That is the question we should ask ourselves any time we find the desires of sin rising in our flesh. We are not under the dominion of sin, or under the law which empowers sin but we are under grace. *"Do you not know that if you surrender yourselves as bond-servants to obey any one, you become the bond-servant of him whom you obey, whether the bond-servant of Sin (with death as the result) or of Duty (resulting in righteousness)? But thanks be to God that though you were once in thralldom to Sin, you have now yielded a hearty obedience to that system of truth in which you have been instructed. You were set free from the tyranny of Sin, and became the bond-servants of Righteousness—."* (Vs 16-18, Weymouth-Trans)

A bond servant is a slave who has been released but has deliberately decided to offer himself back as a slave. We were set free from sin. To offer our members back to sinful passions is to become bond slaves to sin. *"I speak in human terms because of the weakness of your flesh. For just as you presented your members as slaves of uncleanness, and of lawlessness leading to more lawlessness, so now present your members as slaves of righteousness for holiness."* (Vs 19)

The answer to all this is to present our bodies "place near, yield" not to sin but as slaves of righteousness. *"Finally, brethren, whatever things are true, whatever things are noble, whatever things are just, whatever things are pure, whatever things are lovely, whatever things are of good report, if there is any virtue and if there is anything praiseworthy—meditate on these things."* (Phil 4:8)

Grace is not a license to sin but an empowerment to live the life of God, the newness of life which we have been called to, a life where we are fully aware and have conclusively understood that sin no longer has part in our lives. Our old self which accommodated sin and was slave to sin and was under the dominion of sin was crucified at the cross, therefore we can not yield ourselves to sin any more. *"But now having been set free from sin, and having become slaves of God, you have your fruit to holiness, and the end, everlasting life."* (Romans 6:22).

We have been set free from the dominion of sin, transferred from the country of sin and become bond servants to God, we offer ourselves to God and the fruit of this is holiness, God's life eternally. This is the life God wants you to enjoy, a life of holiness without end. *"For the grace of God that brings salvation has appeared to all men, teaching us that, **denying ungodliness and worldly lusts,** we should live soberly, righteously, and godly in the present age, looking for the blessed hope and glorious appearing of our great God and Savior Jesus Christ, who gave Himself for us, that He might redeem us from every lawless deed and purify for Himself His own special people, zealous for good works."* (Titus 2:11-14). The grace of God teaches us to say no to ungodliness, worldly lusts, and lawless deeds and to live soberly, righteously and godly in this age. It does not give us the freedom to walk in the flesh, let us not use our freedom to entertain sin in our lives. (Gal. 5:13).

## Rogue Agent

After understanding all that God has done to liberate us from the power of sin, why do we still find ourselves in the wrong side, why do we find some evil thoughts attacking our minds, why do we see evil desires rising in our members? Paul explains a struggle he encountered in his life before the knowledge of what happened to him on the cross when he was still under the law. *"But sin, taking opportunity by the commandment, produced in me all manner of evil desire. For apart from the law sin was dead. I was alive once without the law, but when the commandment came, sin revived and I died.... For sin, taking occasion by the commandment, deceived me, and by it killed me.... But sin, that it might appear sin, was producing death in me through what is good, so that sin through the commandment might become exceedingly sinful.* "(Romans 7:8-9, 11, 13).

Paul discovered a rogue agent who took opportunity of the commandments to produce all kinds of evil desires in him. This rogue agent called sin was dormant before the commandment came but when the commandment came, this rogue agent revived in the life of Paul. *"But now, it is no longer I who do it, but sin that dwells in me. Now if I do what I will not to do, it is no longer I who do it, but sin that dwells in me."* (Vs 17, 23).

After the fall of Adam, sin got hold of the human body, it couldn't be noticed because sin works well when the law is present. Sin could not be accounted for in the absence of a law. God gave the commandments to reveal sin, so that man could discover this rogue agent that lived in us. God spoke to Cain about this agent, *"you will be accepted if you do what is right. But if you refuse to do what is right, then watch out! Sin is crouching at the door, eager to control you. But you must subdue it and be its master."* (Gen 4:7, NLT). Sin is an organized force complete with desires and an agenda to control and has always sought for an opportunity to manifest its character through us. It mustard the human flesh and dominated the human life.

At the cross, the body which was subject to sin was crucified and died. Remember sin never died, it is the body which sin had dominated, which sin had legal right to operate in through the fall of Adam, it is that body which was crucified. Sin lost its dominion in the human body unless you submit yourself to it. In our study in

Romans 6, Paul tells us what we need to know concerning our victory on the cross over sin. We should not yield, present our members to sin, it no longer has the right to rule in our lives. We were raised to another life in Christ where sin has no dominion over us unless we willingly offer ourselves to sin as bond servants to obey it.

In Romans 7, Paul is not speaking about the life of a believer, a believer in Christ is not under the law. Paul has just told us in Romans 6 that we are not under the law but under grace, the experience he reveals is the life he lived as a Pharisee under the law, he was dead under the law. After salvation Paul discovers this rogue agent was dethroned at the cross. *"for the law of the Spirit of life in Christ Jesus has made me free from the law of sin and death. For what the law could not do in that it was weak through the flesh, God did by sending His own Son in the likeness of sinful flesh, on account of sin: He condemned sin in the flesh, that the righteous requirement of the law might be fulfilled in us who do not walk according to the flesh but according to the Spirit."* (Romans 8:2-4).

The human flesh was completely dominated by sin, we could not get ourselves out of the dominion of sin in our flesh. The wages of sin is death, when sin matures, it gives birth to death. Christ took upon Himself the human body and became sin on the cross, sin demanded death to the human body which was perfectly fulfilled at the cross. Therefore sin has no more claim on the human flesh. A judgement to sin was delivered at the cross, the body which sin subdued was nailed to the cross, Christ did not just remove the cobwebs and let the spider free, He killed the spider, the body of sin. Sin has no more claim on the human body, it operates only if we yield to its lusts and desires. It can not take us captive by force because it has no control unless we let it reign. By Christ dying on the cross for sin, **the righteous requirements of the law were met not by us but in us.** What the law demanded in terms of righteousness was met in us. So we owe the law nothing, we don't have to fulfill anything to prove to the law, its demands were fully met in us.

*"Therefore do not let sin reign in your mortal body, that you should obey it in its lusts..... For sin shall not have dominion over you, for you are not under law but under grace....And having been set free from sin, you became slaves of righteousness.... But now having been set free from sin, and having become slaves of God, you have your fruit to holiness, and the end, everlasting life."* (Rom 6:12, 14, 18, and 22). We can not die again on regard to sin, the body of sin was sentenced on the cross and the gift we have received is eternal life in Christ Jesus. Sin knows its dominance in the human body was broken, the only way it can show its character is by enticing us, by arousing thoughts in our mind to mislead us. The moment you find yourself thinking what is not right you should not blame ourselves, we should know there is another agent called sin which seeks opportunity to control and manifest its character through us.

When a patient goes to a doctor with symptoms of flu, the doctor knows how to differentiate between the patient and the flu that manifests its character through the patient. **He will handle the patient gently but at the same time deal ruthlessly with the flu, at no time does the patient become the flu.** We should make the same distinction, it is not you but the rogue agent bringing evil thoughts and desires to you, you should not allow it to build its nest in your head. Don't let yourself be enticed by placing your members beside what is contrary to your new nature. You died to sin and are alive to God in Christ Jesus,

*"Likewise you also, reckon yourselves* (make a calculation and come to a logical conclusion) *to be dead indeed to sin, but alive to God in Christ Jesus our Lord."* (Rom 6:11). *"From now on, think of it this way: Sin speaks a dead language that means nothing to you; God speaks your mother tongue, and you hang on every word. You are dead to sin and alive to God. That's what Jesus did."* (Message)

**Flesh**
Another prominent agent Paul mentions severally in his writings is the flesh, some translators translated the word flesh to sinful nature. The Greek word used to refer to flesh is the word *"sarx"* which means the flesh or body and sometimes interpreted carnal, not the sinful nature. **The sinful nature was completely dealt with on the cross** *"knowing this, that our old man was crucified with Him, that the body of sin might be done away with, that we should no longer be slaves of sin."* (Rom 6:6). That body which accommodated sin and was subject to sin was crucified on the cross, that's the understanding we should have.

The human flesh having been held captive under sin since the fall of man, has developed sinful tendencies which war against our spiritual man, the flesh has its own lusts which are evident.

*"But put on the Lord Jesus Christ, and make no provision for the flesh, to fulfill its lusts."* (Rom 6:14). *"And those who are Christ's have crucified the flesh with its passions and desires."* (Gal 5:24). *"Among whom also we all once conducted ourselves in the lusts of our flesh, fulfilling the desires of the flesh and of the mind, and were by nature children of wrath, just as the others."* (Eph 2:3)

*"Beloved, I beg you as sojourners and pilgrims, abstain from fleshly lusts which war against the soul,"* (1 Pet 2:11). *"For when they speak great swelling words of emptiness, they allure through the lusts of the flesh, through lewdness, the ones who have actually escaped from those who live in error."* (2 Pet 2:18). *"I say then, Walk in the Spirit, and you shall not fulfill the lust of the flesh. For the flesh lust against the Spirit, and the Spirit against the flesh: and these are contrary to one another: so that you do not do the things that you wish."* (Gal 5:16-17).

In Gal 5:19-, Paul gives us a detailed list of the lusts of the flesh, things which the flesh desires which are contrary to our new nature in Christ. The flesh will always try to manifest itself through our members and take control of our souls. Our soul, that is our mind, will and emotions are always at bay and can either be subjected to the spirit or taken over by the flesh. The soul doesn't contain any spiritual nature in itself, the soul either mirrors the flesh or the spirit. The flesh desire is to rule over our lives and the way to rule our lives is to take over our souls. The flesh reveals a way to think and walk.

*"For those who live according to the flesh set their minds on the things of the flesh, but those who live according to the Spirit, the things of the Spirit. For to be carnally minded is death, but to be spiritually minded is life and peace. Because the carnal mind is enmity against God; for it is not subject to the law of God, nor indeed can be. So then, those who are in the flesh cannot please God. But you are not in the flesh but in the Spirit, if indeed the Spirit of God dwells in you. Now if anyone does not have the Spirit of Christ, he is not His. "* (Rom 8:5-9).

Paul concludes by letting us know we are not in the flesh but in the Spirit, we are not under obligation to obey the desires of the flesh which are not subject to God, we have crucified the flesh with its desires and passions, (Gal 5:24).

*"Therefore, brethren, we are debtors—not to the flesh, to live according to the flesh. For if you live according to the flesh you will die; but if by the Spirit you put to death the deeds of the body, you will live. For as many as are led by the Spirit of God, these are sons of God. "* (Rom 8:12-14). Our only obligation is to put to death the deeds of the flesh by the Spirit who lives in us.

Remember in Rom 8:3 Paul tells us how sin was condemned in the flesh, through the death of Christ on the cross. We are now not dealing with sin in this chapter eight but the pollution caused by sin in our members after years of living under sin. We should put to an end these fleshly desires which war against our spirit by walking in the Spirit, for all of us who are sons have the Spirit of God. If we subject our lives to the flesh, the results will be obvious, we shall manifest what is contrary to our true nature yet sin has been dealt with on the cross, but the pollution of sin still remains in our flesh.

*"I say then: Walk in the Spirit, and you shall not fulfill the lust of the flesh. For the flesh lusts against the Spirit, and the Spirit against the flesh; and these are contrary to one another, so that you do not do the things that you wish. But if you are led by the Spirit, you are not under the law."* (Gal 5:16-17). *"But the fruit of the Spirit is love, joy, peace, longsuffering, kindness, goodness, faithfulness, gentleness, self–control. Against such there is no law. And those who are Christ's have crucified the flesh with its passions and desires. If we live in the Spirit, let us also walk in the Spirit."* (Vs 22-25).

The Spiritual life we have received does not give the flesh opportunity to manifest its character, as long as we know we are in the Spirit and live our lives by the Spirit, the works of the flesh shall have no room in our lives. The Spiritual life we live is not subject to any rules or laws, there is no law against love, joy peace, kindness. We have been called to a life of liberty from every obligation of the law and the flesh.

God has transferred us from a life dominated and empowered by the lusts of the flesh to a life dominated and empowered by the Spirit of God and the fruit of the Spirit should spontaneously and effortlessly manifest through us. **To try to manifest the life of God by your own efforts is like a car trying to defy the law of gravity and fly**. Whatever speed the car accelerates, it will not be able to defy the law of gravity, it is subject to that law and can not fly. Even if we remove all obstacles of traffic lights and bumps and drive the car in a runway it will not fly, it is still subject to the law of gravity. For you to fly you need an airplane which is fitted with an aircraft engine which has the capability of defying the law of gravity. The law of aerodynamics defies the law of gravity.

All your self efforts can not help you defy the law of sin and death, there is only one law which is superior to the law of sin and death, it is the law of the Spirit of life. When we are in Christ the law of sin and death has no power over us. Like one who is in an aircraft powered by the engines, the law of gravity is defied. The law of the Spirit of life has given us victory over the law of sin and death.

The flesh is not necessarily tuned to evil, there are religious tendencies also manifested by the flesh. Paul reveals his zeal for the law, *"though I also might have confidence in the flesh. If anyone else thinks he may have confidence in the flesh, I more so: circumcised the eighth day, of the stock of Israel, of the tribe of Benjamin, a Hebrew of the Hebrews; concerning the law, a Pharisee; concerning zeal, persecuting the church; concerning the righteousness which is in the law, blameless. "* (Phil 3:4-6).

The flesh gave him confidence to boast of his achievements which come by his own efforts apart from God. This is one of the common tendencies of the flesh which does not appear to be evil

160

but gives room for pride in putting confidence on you apart from God. There are many people today who are held by the pride of flesh that they fail to submit to God's purpose for their lives, they have put their confidence in what they have achieved through their flesh.

The flesh will not lead you always to what is evil, the Galatians were rebuked by Paul for trying to improve themselves by their own efforts. They had began well in the Spirit but were now seeking self improvement through the flesh. *"How foolish can you be? After starting your Christian lives in the Spirit, why are you now trying to become perfect by your own human effort?"* (Gal 3:3, NLT).

This is common not only to the Galatians but even to the believers today, we begin our journey by faith then we try every day to improve ourselves by our own efforts. We want to receive acceptance from God by trying to improve ourselves without relying on the Spirit of God. There are myriads of believers who believe by their commitment to God or to church or their giving and religious commitment they become more righteous and this makes God more inclined to them. By their prayers and fasting they can turn God's mind to them. Even unbelievers believe they can earn salvation through their prayers and generosity. This is self improvement flesh which is contrary to God's will. There is no other sacrifice better than the cross that will ever move God, God has already moved to us and no any other sacrifice we can offer which can change God's mind about us.

Note that the Corinthian church was struggling with sin more than the Galatian church, Paul at no moment called the Corinthians fools, sin can be dealt with by God's grace, in fact he called them saints, he spoke of good things about them. But when the Galatians tried to improve themselves through the flesh, he referred to them as fools, that's how much God hates self improvement by the flesh. This is what got Adam into trouble, trying to be like God by his own efforts. We preach to unbelievers to improve themselves first before believing in Christ, they should stop smoking, drinking and then come to church. That is self improvement flesh contrary to the saving power of the gospel. **The gospel advocates salvation by faith in Christ not self improvement.**

### Behavior

One would ask a question, what entails the behavior verses we have in the epistles, should we obey them as the laws to govern our Christian lives or should we fail to obey them, shall we encounter the wrath of God? The rules we find in the epistles are just a reminder to us of what our nature is, they remind us of the will of God for us. We have already received a new heart and a new Spirit. *"I will give you a new heart and put a new spirit within you; I will take the heart of stone out of your flesh and give you a heart of flesh. "I will put My Spirit within you and cause you to walk in my statutes, and you will keep my judgments and do them. "* (Ezek 36:26-27).

This is a promise which has been fulfilled in our day, we are not like the old covenant Jews who had hearts of stone and could not obey the commandments. God has put His laws into our hearts, and His Spirit causes us to walk in them. The law seeks behavior modification, grace transforms the heart. These rules in the epistles echo what already is true in our hearts. (Heb 8:10).

*"Since, then, we do not have the excuse of ignorance, everything—and I do mean everything—connected with that old way of life has to go. It's rotten through and through. Get rid of it! And then take on an entirely new way of life—a God-fashioned life, a life renewed from the inside and working itself into your conduct as God accurately reproduces his character in you. What this adds up to, then, is this: no more lies, no more pretense. Tell your neighbor the truth. In Christ's body we're all connected to each other, after all. When you lie to others, you end up lying to yourself."* (Eph 4:22-25, Message).

It is God reproducing His character through us, *"it is God who works in us to will and to do according to His good pleasure,"* (Phil 2:13). These are expected of us, they point to us our identity as the sons of God. They are reminders to what already has been instituted in us by the Holy Spirit, we are to manifest them effortlessly just as a tree manifests its character by bearing fruits.

Consider a prostitute who has been all her life on the streets often arrested for prostitution, charged, fined and released. One day an officer approaches her and informs her the king has ordered she will never be arrested again nor charged for prostitution, will this stop her from prostituting? No, it won't. But suppose the officer informs her from that day she will be married to the king and live in the palace with the king, will she have the desire to go back to streets? Definitely not. That's what has to get in the mind of every believer and they will have no reason to go to the streets again.

What about if we don't obey, or live according to these rules as believers, should we expect the wrath of God as it was in the Old Testament? Should we expect curses from God following us? No, there is no punishment from God, no curses to follow us. Paul tells us twice *"All things are lawful for me," but not all things are beneficial. "All things are lawful for me," but I will not be dominated by anything."* (1 Cor 6:12, 10:23).

We are not under the bondage of any system of behavior laws. The fruit of the Spirit is our standard of life which we effortlessly manifest. All things are permissible but not all things are beneficial, we should look at what is beneficial to us as believers inline with our new nature. But what if we continue in this way of life which is contrary to our new nature are there consequences? Of course yes, there are consequences for our irresponsible behavior, we will fall on the wrong side of the law of the land and the consequences are clear, we will hurt our fellow believers by being irresponsible in our relationships.

A brother who goes around peddling lies will find himself out of fellowship with his friends. He will loose trust among believers and will never be taken serious. Sin in itself is a torture, even if God does not punish you, sin in itself is a punishment, it will make your life miserable and torture you, you won't have piece in your life. Paul urged the Corinthians to deliver such a believer to the devil to be tormented in his flesh that his spirit may be saved (1 Cor 5:5). To whoever you offer your members to obey you become a slave to (Rom 6:16). When you are a slave to sin you are equally the devil's slave who is the author of sicknesses and all manner of evil. You know what to expect because the devil is generous in doing his work, you will face all manner of torment. After getting this knowledge it will be irresponsible of us to continue in our former life. There is no other blood which can cleanse us again, we were cleansed once and we remain cleansed, what remains is a miserable life of torture under slavery to sin, sin is a bad master, it will inflict all kind of pain to you.

Paul urges believers in Corinth (1 Cor 5:11) not to associate with any brother who is sexually immoral, or covetous, or an idolater, or a drunkard, or a reviler, or an extortioner. In fact Paul makes it much serious by urging them not even to eat with such a person. Therefore for us to continue in irresponsible behavior deliberately there are consequences. But to him who changes his mind from these evil practices definitely he should be restored to the fellowship of believers.

The grace of God teaches us to say no to ungodliness and worldly passions and to live soberly, righteously and godly in this present age (Titus 2:11). Sin is contrary to who we are. After the harsh later which Paul wrote to the Corinthians, he writes again to celebrate the outcome which it caused among them. *"Now I rejoice, not in your grief, but because the grief led to repentance; for you sorrowed with a godly sorrow, which prevented you from*

165

*receiving injury from us in any respect. For godly sorrow produces repentance leading to salvation, a repentance not to be regretted; but the sorrow of the world finally produces death. For mark the effects of this very thing—your having sorrowed with a godly sorrow—what earnestness it has called forth in you, what eagerness to clear yourselves, what indignation, what alarm, what longing affection, what jealousy, what meting out of justice! You have completely wiped away reproach from yourselves in the matter."* (1 Cor 7:9-11 Weymouth)

*"I am jealous over you with God's own jealousy. For I have betrothed you to Christ to present you to Him like a faithful bride to her one husband."* (2 Cor 11:2, Weymouth). This was the passion that Paul was moved with in his ministry. He could tell us there is no condemnation to him who is in Christ and at the same time rebuke with strong words those who took advantage of God's grace to walk in sin. Any believer who says he is under grace and walks in sin is not under grace because God's grace does not promote sin, it's the law which promotes sin, grace empowers righteousness in us. As Francois du Toit says, 'realizing and esteeming your true origin and nature makes anything inconsistent with your original design unattractive.'[1]

Let us manifest what we are, we are eagles not chicken, let's not try to manifest chicken behavior after we've known we are eagles, let us hear the voice of the mother eagle calling us from the clouds and let us soar high in newness of life. *"**Awake to righteousness, and do not sin;** for some do not have the knowledge of God. I speak this to your shame."* (1 Cor 15:34).

---

*1, Francois du Toit, God believes in you, pg 31'*

*"Therefore be imitators of God as dear children. And walk in love, as Christ also has loved us and given Himself for us, an offering and a sacrifice to God for a sweet–smelling aroma. But fornication and all uncleanness or covetousness, let it not even be named among you, as is fitting for saints; neither filthiness, nor foolish talking, nor coarse jesting, which are not fitting, but rather giving of thanks. For this you know, that no fornicator, unclean person, nor covetous man, who is an idolater, has any inheritance in the kingdom of Christ and God. Let no one deceive you with empty words, for because of these things the wrath of God comes upon the sons of disobedience. Therefore do not be partakers with them. For you were once darkness, but now you are light in the Lord. Walk as children of light (for the fruit of the Spirit is in all goodness, righteousness, and truth), finding out what is acceptable to the Lord. And have no fellowship with the unfruitful works of darkness, but rather expose them. For it is shameful even to speak of those things which are done by them in secret"* (Eph 5:1-12). We are not the sons of disobedience (unbelievers) but sons of God, we follow and manifest the life of God.

Someone would ask what about Hebrews 12, *"And you have forgotten the exhortation which speaks to you as to sons: "My son, do not despise the chastening of the LORD, Nor be discouraged when you are rebuked by Him; For whom the LORD loves He chastens, And scourges every son whom He receives."* (Heb 12:5-6). The Greek word translated to chasten is the word 'paideuo' (were we get the english word pediatrician) which means child training, to be instructed or taught or learn, molding the character of others by reproof and admonition using words. It does not mean punishment.

We are sons, therefore God deals with us as sons, no father hurts his child in the name of training them. Our heavenly Father trains us in the way of righteousness through His word. If we earthly fathers don't hurt our children why should you imagine God causing a serious road accident to train His child lessons? In the Old Testament God chastised His people through punishment for their sins that is if they failed to repent and continued in evil. God's grace had not been revealed. (Lev 26:28) Christ bore our punishment why should we be punished again for sin? When God deals with us in the New Testament, He deals with children and has poured His grace on us.

When **Solomon was constructing the temple no sound of hammer or chisel was heard in the construction site.** All the stones were shaped in the quarry. (1 Kings 6:7) The quarry was a picture of the cross. We as living stones being built into a holy temple of the Lord (1 Pet 2:4-5) were shaped at the cross of Jesus, that is where all the chastisement for our peace was done. We are complete in Him, we only grow in the knowledge of how complete we are.

### Hazard
Should we turn our pulpits to places of exposing sin, teaching about sin and showing the believers every Sunday the sinful life? It's unfortunate that in most of our fellowships we have turned the pulpits to be a shop to market the works of flesh, this Sunday we

preach about fornication, the following Sunday about covetousness, the following Sunday we preach about lust of the flesh, the following Sunday we teach about lying, the following Sunday disobedience.

We have turned the pulpit to be a warning ground about sin, we raise the red flag every week, we have made sin the core thing of our everyday preaching. These are believers washed by the blood who are filled with the Spirit of God, who have been delivered from the power of sin, why subject them to sin again every week? We can not put a New Testament believer in the same place as the Old Testament believer who never had the experience of the Holy Spirit living in them, they were more vulnerable to sin and therefore required all warnings against sinning, but that does not apply to us today. Let them know their position in Christ, what has been freely given to them, the victory they have over sin, their new nature in Christ. Help them discover where they are, the throne room realities, the divine life they have. Give them the knowledge of how righteous they have become, they will manifest righteousness. But if every Sunday they learn how sinful they are, sin will manifest in their lives. As a man thinks so is he.

A man once gave me a story of a life he went through. He was in a relationship with a woman he really never loved, this woman was a real torture in his life. She was called Shelly. Shelly made life very difficult for this man, she could often beat up this man until he was forced to break up completely with Shelly. He fell in love with another woman called Angela.

Angela has been the love of his life, she has been everything this man needed, very cooperative, understanding and caring, they lived very well. But one of this man's best friend began visiting him, always reminding him about Shelly and telling him how Shelly admires him, what Shelly has been planning for him and asking him to be very careful about Shelly. This man began having memories of Shelly, he become more worried and anxious about Shelly. He could no longer walk free but tried by all means not to fall in the path of Shelly. He had forgotten about her and was leaving a good life with Angela but it's no more, he is more worried of Shelly than he loves Angela.

This is what we do when we awaken sin in our pulpits, we were once married to sin but we got a divorce from sinful life, to market sin every Sunday is to awaken the memories of a partner we already divorced. These memories hinder our walk with our new found lover. We make people more conscious of sin than of Jesus. Teaching about sin is not the solution, let the people be taught the right thing, they will easily know when the wrong one appears. **A bank teller is taught how the real notes look like and how they feel so that anytime they handle a fake note they will easily know it is fake.** Let the truth of the gospel be the motivation of our teaching. Truth is not found in the transgression. It is truth that sets free from sin.

## Law of Perfect Liberty.

The New Testament introduces a new concept in the life of the believer different from what was the norm in the Old Testament. *"Therefore lay aside all filthiness and overflow of wickedness, and receive with meekness the implanted word, which is able to save your souls. But be doers of the word, and not hearers only, deceiving yourselves. For if anyone is a hearer of the word and not a doer, he is like a man observing his natural face in a mirror; for he observes himself, goes away, and immediately forgets what kind of man he was. But he who looks into the perfect law of liberty and continues in it, and is not a forgetful hearer but a doer of the work, this one will be blessed in what he does."* (James 1:21-25, NLT)

James says we receive with meekness the implanted (engrafted) word which is able to save our souls, we be doers of the word and not only hearers. In the Old Testament, the Jews were instructed by God to obey His word. The word obey in Hebrew is the word "*Shawmer*," It means to '*guard, protect, to attend to.*' God instructed the Jews to protect the word, to guard it and to attend to it. The word and the people were not one, they could loose the word, therefore they were instructed to make sure the word was protected through obeying.

James tells us to be doers of the word. The word doer is a Greek word "*poyaytace*" it means '*maker, producer, author.*' **In the New Testament we don't guard the word; we are the producers, the authors and makers of the word.** The word has become one with us. God said He will put His laws in us, we are not separated from the word, we produce the word from within us. We act what is in us. We receive with meekness the engrafted word. The word has been engrafted and joined with us, the word lives in us. We are the offspring of the word, we have been born again of the incorruptible seed of the word of God. (1 Pet 1:23). If anyone hears the word but does not do (produce) the word is like a man who looks at his face in a mirror and goes away forgetting (neglectful, no longer caring) what he saw. The word mirrors you, it simply means the word shows you who you are, it reveals to you your true self. So whoever looks at the word and does the opposite has forgotten what he saw in the word. God has painted a picture of your life in the word. The entire Bible is about Christ and all about Christ is about you. Christ came knowing what had been written about him and He walked in it, also we should walk in what has been written about us.

He who looks at the word (the perfect law of liberty), the word which speaks your freedom. Freedom from all that is negative about your life, what God has not intended for you, and continues in it being not a forgetful hearer but a doer of the work shall be blessed in all he does. James says he who looks (Greek "*parakupto*"), it means '*to bend over so as to pear within and study with microscopic scrutiny.*' He implies to study the word with a keen interest to see something in the word. And continues in it (Greek "*Parameno*"), '*to stay under the influence of the word, to remain under the magnetic pool of the word.*' You read or hear the word and you remain under the force of what you have seen, you are captivated by the picture you saw in the word, you produce what you saw, this man shall be blessed in all he does, all he produces, all that comes from him.

This is the perfect law of liberty which gives us freedom from all contradictions of life. The law of Moses showed us how sinful we were, the gospel shows us how righteous we have become. A man who is under the influence of drugs, has struggled all his life to get himself out of this strong addiction hears the word, is captivated by the reality of that life and gets the picture of himself free from drugs, that is the end of drugs holding him captive.

Get the picture of your liberty from the word, remain under that influence of what you saw no matter how long it takes and the results are obvious. Anything that has taken us captive, the freedom is in what the word paints about you. The solution already exists in the word. If it is diseases, see the picture the word paints about the whole you, if its poverty see the picture of the successful you painted by Him becoming poor for you to enjoy His riches. He who supplies all your needs according to His riches in glory.

The Bible is just a book like any other, it carries no magic but **when the living word in you gets connected to the written word on scripture it gives life to the written word** and the results will be evident. Life begins manifesting from what has always been there common to you. You get a fresh understanding and the results are life changing. David speaks of this blessing, *"Bless the LORD, O my soul, And forget not all His benefits: Who forgives all your iniquities, Who heals all your diseases, Who redeems your life from destruction, Who crowns you with loving-kindness and tender mercies, Who satisfies your mouth with good things, So that your youth is renewed like the eagle's."* (Psalms 103:2-5)

## New Commandment.

*"But when the Pharisees heard that He had silenced the Sadducees, they gathered together. Then one of them, a lawyer, asked Him a question, testing Him, and saying, "Teacher, which is the great commandment in the law?" Jesus said to him, "You shall love the LORD your God with all your heart, with all your soul, and with all your mind.' "This is the first and great commandment."And the second is like it: 'You shall love your neighbor as yourself.' "On these two commandments hang all the Law and the Prophets. "* (Matt 22:34-40).

Jesus summarized the Ten Commandments into two laws which were part of the Old Testament laws. Loving God with all your heart, with all your soul and with all your mind (Deut 6:5) and loving your neighbor as yourself (Lev 19:18). These are not new commandments for the church to keep, they are part of the old system. To love your brother as you love yourself may not be very practical, there are people in our society who do not appreciate themselves, others commit suicide, they will automatically reciprocate the same to their neighbors, and eventually it will not fulfill the Spirit of Love.

Loving God with your entire being was not possible, as we have seen there are rogue agents in our lives who are opposed to God and the ways of God. How do you love God if you don't have that love in you, you don't have the fruit of the Spirit? This was the message of Jesus to the Pharisees who thought they could be justified by keeping the law, which as we saw earlier was impossible.

Jesus command to the disciples, *"A new commandment I give unto you, that ye love one another; as I have loved you, that ye also love one another. By this shall all men know that ye are my disciples, if ye have love one to another."* (John 13:34-35). If we love one another as Christ has loved us, we will be ready to lay down our lives for our fellow brothers. To love one another, we should first see and understand how Christ has loved us and receive this love. When we receive the love of God then shall we be able to manifest what is in us.

The believers today struggle loving one another because they have not seen and comprehended how Christ loved them unconditionally nor received this unconditional love. We put limits to our friends because we think also God's love to us is conditional. Once we see and fathom the unconditional love of God then we will love our brothers unconditionally and also love God back because He first loved us.

*"And this is his commandment, that we should believe on the name of his Son Jesus Christ, and love one another, as he gave us commandment."* (1 John 3:23). *"We love Him because He first loved us. If someone says, "I love God," and hates his brother, he is a liar; for he who does not love his brother whom he has seen, how can he love God whom he has not seen? And this commandment we have from Him: that he who loves God must love his brother also."* (1 John 4:19-21). God did not love us because we were lovable but because He is love and if love dwells in us we ought to manifest the same. **The best way to love God is to love your brother**, God dwells in your brother, and to love

your brother is to love God. Let's allow the fruit of the Spirit, Love, to manifest through us, it's already in us.

*"Beloved, let us love one another, for love is of God; and everyone who loves is born of God and knows God. He who does not love does not know God, for God is love. In this the love of God was manifested toward us, that God has sent His only begotten Son into the world, that we might live through Him. In this is love, not that we loved God, but that He loved us and sent His Son to be the propitiation for our sins. Beloved, if God so loved us, we also ought to love one another. No one has seen God at any time. If we love one another, God abides in us, and His love has been perfected in us. By this we know that we abide in Him, and He in us, because He has given us of His Spirit."* (1 John 4:7-13). It's a new effortless life empowered by the Spirit of God. We only bring out what already is in us.

# *EIGHT*

## MIND-SET

A friend once narrated to us a story about a Pretorian eagle. My friend had gone for honeymoon in Mpumalanga, one of the tour guides narrated a story to them of an eagle which had been recently released. A zoo keeper captured an eagle ten years ago and kept it in his zoo, he could make good money from tourists who come to see the eagle in a zoo. The black eagle was one meter tall and had a wingspan of 2.3 meters. It attracted so many tourists to the zoo. One time the animal conservation officials visited the zoo and found this eagle. They filed a case in court seeking the release of this eagle back to the wild. The date for hearing of the case was set and judgement was delivered. The judge declared the eagle was not meant for the cage but for the wild therefore in his ruling he set a date for the release of this eagle.

On the said date, many journalists, animal conservation activists and all interested parties were gathered to witness this spectacular sight of the release of the eagle after ten years of being kept in a cage. The cage was loaded onto a truck and driven to the mountains, they lowered the cage from the truck and opened the door of the cage.

To their surprise the eagle refused to get out of the cage, they had to push it out of the cage. The crowds were full of cheers shouting freedom for the eagle. Unfortunately the eagle did not fly away, it never realized it was free at last. Though the eagle was out of the cage but the eagles mind was still caged. The cameras were rolling waiting to capture the first adventure of this eagle, but nothing happened.

After a long wait, all the audience lost hope of seeing the eagle fly away to the skies, they were held in a discussion what to do next. It was getting late and to leave that eagle out there they knew was disastrous, it could easily be devoured by other animals, to take it back to the cage posed a legal challenge, it would contravene the court ruling. While they were still held up in discussion, another eagle passed above the mountains chanting some eagle noise, suddenly the eyes of this eagle brightened and it began gazing at the clouds, without any warning, or lessons to fly it took off to the skies.

The children of Israel found themselves in the same state as this eagle, they had been delivered from Egypt with a mighty hand of God. In Egypt they had conformed to slavery, they were used to being ordered around, being under command, and being shown what to do always. An average slave had totally lost control over his own life. They completely depended on instructions from their task masters. Now for the first time they found themselves free from their task masters and now they had all their lives to themselves.

They were the one's to control and manage their own affairs and this was not easy to many of them. The challenge of freedom was eating up their minds. They even suggested it was better while they were still in Egypt, they used to receive everything free from their task masters. **They were out of Egypt but their minds were still trapped in the systems of Egypt,** just as this eagle which was released from the cage but its mind was still caged. It was easy to remove the eagle from the cage than to remove the cage from the mind of the eagle.

We encounter the same challenge of freedom today. Our lives were patterned by the sinful lusts we used to live in and the religious system we were raised under. We were taught of a harsh God who hates sinners terribly. A God who is so difficult to please and we ought to work so hard to win His favor, so that He may bless us. Our lives were patterned by our fleshly desires; we were subject to the cravings of sin and our flesh. In our religious lives, we were taught we had to work out our own righteousness by our good works.

We lived in fear of losing our salvation, it made us to be so careful not to break the commandments in the Bible, we had no freedom, we were under bondage to try and please God. We patterned our lives under the old covenant system, we believed in a God who appears and disappears at will. Like the caged eagle, this became our cage locking our minds, they become strong holds to us. We are out of the cage but our minds are still caged by our sinful lives or our religious lifestyle.

**Thoughts.**
What you hear is what makes you to be who you are, what you hear is what controls your life, even circumstances speak to us. If

you have given yourself to listening to messages of condemnation that's how your life will be patterned, guilt and condemnation will be the order of the day to you. If you submit your ears and eyes to unprofitable lusts of the flesh that's what you will manifest daily. **'Words are spirit vehicles,'[1] the words you hear have direct influence to your life**. A man is happy cracking jokes with his friends, he receives a phone call and immediately his face changes and his mood changes instantly, the news he received through the phone conversation has taken over his mind and eventually affected his mood.

'Seed stores the life energy and the genetic detail of a plant species in much the same way thoughts and concepts are concealed in languages and words.'[2] The words we speak reveal concepts which have been stored in our minds. We believe God leaves us and we speak words which reveal the same. The words we hear activate the energy fields of our minds and controls our ultimate behavior. These words become thoughts which activate the energy fields of the mind which dictate the outcome of our day to day experience. Cultivate a thought pattern through the words you hear that pictures the ultimate life you want. '**A mans life will be of the character of his thoughts.'** (John G. Lake)

'Our thoughts are silent words which only God and we can hear, but those words affect our inner man, joy and attitude in life.'[3] *"Now to Him who is able to do exceedingly abundantly above all that we ask or think, according to the power that works in us"* (Ephe 3:20). It suggests our thoughts can be our answered prayers, we should take care which thoughts we allow in our

*1, 2, 3, Francois du Toit, God believes in you. pg 14,15,27.*

minds. *"Guard your heart above all else, for it determines the course of your life."* (Prov 4:23, NLT). The word heart suggests the soul of man where our thoughts, will and emotions come from. Your thoughts determine the outcome of your life. 'Your thoughts leads the way to your spirit, the inner core of your being, here the core of your origin and spirit identity is stored in much the same way as the cells in your body preserve the DNA code of genetic identity'[4].

'**Your thoughts are your sanctuary, your sacred space and secret place**'[5]. That is the place you ought to guard above all else, 'A thought may remain  secret and invisible for sometime, but it will inevitably affect your conversation, mood and health. It is no secret that negative thought pattern is often the cause of depression. Your behavior whether it is your body language will often betray your thoughts. An individual's attitude and mood can transmit an invisible energy that influences others'[6]. The kids and their mother were having a good time in the house sharing their meals, suddenly there was a knock at the door, one of the boys opened the door and their father gets in. From the looks of his face they could  tell all was not well, all the laughter went quiet and all their faces changed expecting to hear the bad news from their father, that's how one's attitude can completely change an environment.

The thoughts of God have become the thoughts of men, we have the mind of Christ and have received the Spirit of God that we should access the secrets of God. No one knows the thoughts of a man except the spirit in him, so are the thoughts of God, we access them through His Spirit. We limit ourselves by being trapped in the fleshly mind.

## Transformed

Paul addresses to a greater length the need for our minds to be transformed. **You are a spiritual being and your spirit is not subject to change**. What you are in your spirit is a complete package of what God has for us, we don't reduce or increase in our inner man. The fullness of God dwells in your spirit. The seed of God is in your spirit, all the treasure of wisdom and knowledge are locked up in your spirit. Man has a spirit, soul and body. Your spirit is mature and complete but your mind which forms the soul needs to be transformed from the previous pattern of life to conform to what you are in the spirit. Your mind, moods, feelings and circumstances are bound to change. To grasp all we are in our spirit being, we should allow our minds to be transformed to what is true in our spirit. The soul has nothing spiritual in itself. It depends on where you tune it, it will either yield to your spirit or to the flesh. The flesh as we have seen earlier has been contaminated by sin already, our soul can submit to the flesh or the spirit. A renewed mind conquers the space that was previously occupied by worthless pursuits.

Many Christians still believe we have to undergo a process of sanctification or a process of cleansing so that one time we will be complete and pure without blemish. But the question I normally ask, what if you die before the process is complete, do you go to heaven half sanctified and cleansed? The word sanctification in Greek is the word '*Hagiazo*,' It means to 'dedicate, to separate or set apart for God, or to purify, make conformable.' Christ in His prayer in John 17:19 sanctified Himself that we may be sanctified. We were sanctified in His sanctification. He sanctified Himself on our behalf or for the sake of us. 1 Cor 1:30 tells us "*It is of God are we in Christ who has been made our wisdom, our righteousness, our sanctification and redemption.*" Sanctification is a person, Christ is our sanctification. By the virtue of His abiding in us we have God's sanctification, we are already sanctified. "*And such were some of you, but you were washed, but you were sanctified, but you were justified in the name of the Lord Jesus Christ and in the Spirit of our God.*" (1 Cor 6:11). "*By which will we have been sanctified through the offering of the body of Jesus Christ once for all.*" (Heb 10:10). (Also in Acts 20:32, 26:18, 1 Cor 1:2).

'*Arise and shine for your light has come,*' **light does not create anything in us, it only helps us to see what already is in us and true in our lives.** The light of God's word helps us to realize how complete we are. Col 2:10 tells us "*we are complete in Him who is the head of all principality and power.*" We do not grow towards completeness but we grow in the knowledge of how complete we are. The word complete is the Greek word '*pleroo*' It means 'to abound, liberally supplied, fill to the brim, complete in every aspect, to render perfect.' There is no more additions God has to do in us. "*Don't copy the behavior and customs of this world, but let God transform you into a new person by changing the way you think. Then you will learn to know God's will for you, which is good and pleasing and perfect.*" (Rom 12: 2, NLT)

Transform is a Greek word *"metomorphoo"* from where we get the English word metamorphosis. When a caterpillar undergoes the process of metamorphosis and becomes a butterfly, it will not become a caterpillar again. When our minds are transformed we will not go back to our former ways which were energized by our thinking patterns which become attitudes in our lives. A thought often entertained becomes a footpath in the field of imagination, we imagine those thoughts and finally we do what we have imagined. Our minds are to be made new by hearing what is true to our lives and we will easily conform to the will of God. Our lives were formerly engineered by the lusts of the flesh, we can not go that way again, we should not allow ourselves to conform to the former life of the cage but to our new identity in Christ.

In psychology which is a scientific study of mental processes and behavior, human behavior is mostly influenced by belief system according to most of the theories. In therapy sessions a therapist will have to identify the belief system of the client if it's the one causing them emotional disturbance. The therapist disputes the irrational thoughts caused by the wrong belief replacing irrational with rational thoughts and thereby the client experiences new set of feelings. The central issue is how clients can become aware of their self defeating philosophies, can challenge and act against them. The client develops a rational philosophy of life so that in future they are not victims of irrational beliefs. This is what believers have to do. To challenge their self defeating philosophies which are contrary to their new nature. We need therapy by the word of God to counter our self defeating beliefs. This is cognitive restructuring by the Word.

A mind that has not been transformed will hold you hostage to your former life. Just like the Israelites experience, though they were free from Egypt yet there minds were still captured by the Egyptian experience. We fail to grasp the blessings of God in our lives due to our untransformed minds. We should tune our minds to the reality of what the word says has happened in us. We need to understand we are blessed and allow our minds to picture how blessed we are. We need to understand we are forgiven and allow our minds to picture how forgiven we already are. We need to know we are dead to our former life and allow our minds to picture how dead we are and alive to our new self. Seed which fell on the dry land had the same potential as the seed that fell on good ground. You prepare the soil of your mind and the seed which is God's word brings the maximum harvest.

Like our eagle, its mind was still caged even after being released from the cage, it heard the voice of the free eagle and realigned its mind to the former experience of a free eagle and immediately it was free again to fly. We likewise should align our mind to the free life we have received in Christ. We should hear the voice of the free eagle Christ Jesus and realign our minds to His voice.

We have been redeemed, justified, sanctified, made righteous and blessed with every spiritual blessing in Christ yet our minds haven't comprehended this reality. Many believers still believe there are curses for them if they fail to keep the law yet the Bible clearly says how Christ was hanged on a tree to take away all the curses for us. Jesus could have died any death, He could have been speared to death, or stoned to death, or beheaded, but He had to face the cross according to Deut 21:23 and become a curse, to deal with the curse which was brought by not keeping the law. Now we have the privilege to enjoy the blessings of Abraham upon us who don't keep the law. Like a small rudder steers and dictates a massive vessel, so our thoughts and conversation about ourselves dictate our destiny on the ocean of life.

**Strongholds**

The teachings we have received in our religious backgrounds have formed thinking patterns which in turn have become strongholds or mind-sets. They have become part of our life, and control our attitude and behavior. We imagine strongholds to be somewhere in the air, but Paul speaks of strongholds as thoughts, arguments or reasoning. *"for walking in the flesh, not according to the flesh do we war, for the weapons of our warfare are not fleshly, but powerful to God for bringing down of strongholds, reasoning bringing down, and every high thing lifted up against the knowledge of God, and bringing into captivity every thought to the obedience of the Christ,"* (2 Cor 10:3-6, YLT)

Other versions use opinion and arguments, all these have their residence in the human mind. Our war is in the mind, once we deal with these strongholds in our minds, we will be victorious but as long as we are still held captive by these opinions, thoughts, reasoning and arguments which are contrary to the knowledge of God about us or the mind of Christ, we will not know God's will for us. Even repentance involves a change of mind. *"Whose minds the god of this age has blinded, who do not believe, lest the light of the gospel of the glory of Christ, who is the image of God, should shine on them."* (2 Cor 4:4). The devil has blinded the minds of unbelievers, the mind is the key part of our being, it is key in enjoying the life of God. The mind determines how effective and enjoyable life will be. We have seen people who are blind succeeding in life, we have seen people who lack limbs in their bodies succeeding in life, but we are yet to see anyone psychotic who could achieve success in life.

**Darkness does not erase the truth, it only hides that which light reveals.** Darkness is not a force but the absence of light, we have all seen generators which generate electricity for light but we have never seen darkness generators. The god of this world has blinded (darkened) the minds of unbelievers but the light of the gospel drives this darkness from their minds and they discover who they are. Our mind is the most essential part in our human lives and our Christian walk. Whatever controls the mind controls the individual. Sin is after the control of your mind, the flesh is after the control of the mind and the Spirit of God seeks the attention of your mind.

*"And be renewed in the spirit of your mind, and that you put on the new man which was created according to God, in true righteousness and holiness."* (Eph 4:23). Paul says we should be renewed in the spirit of our mind. The word renew is the word renovate. A house renovated maintains the same structure but everything which was inside is replaced. It is done a new though

not demolished. We should renovate our minds by God's truth, get rid of all the religious garbage and fill your mind with what is true about you. The gospel is what makes our minds new; the understanding of the gospel brings real transformation in our minds. If you pattern your mind according to the Old Testament lifestyle, the New Testament will remain a farfetched dream, you will be longing and waiting for one day in heaven to enjoy what you ought to enjoy in this present life.

Eph 6:11 tells us " *put on the whole armor of God that ye may be able to stand against the wiles of the devil.*" The devil uses cunningness, lies and craftiness. All these are deceptions. So our real battle is not with a powerful enemy with strong power opposing us but a defeated enemy who has devised lies and he uses them to counter every weapon we have. Our minds should be transformed to be able to withstand his lies by the truth of the Word of God. Lies are only conquered by truth. He lies to us about salvation, our righteousness, our weapons and all others.

**Many of us are left praying for the second coming of Christ yet we have failed to enjoy the victory He won for us in His coming**. We fail to enjoy what already has been won for us. Your mind is like your operating system, if your computer has a windows xp then you should expect it to function as an xp is programmed. If you need it to give you the results of a windows vista it will be impossible. Change the operating system of your mind by yielding to truth and you will experience the results you need.

*"Be renewed in your innermost mind!* (***Pondering the truth about you as it is displayed in Christ***) *will cause you to be completely reprogrammed in the way you think about yourself!* (***Notice that Paul does not say, 'Renew your minds!' This transformation happens in the spirit of your mind, awakened by truth in a much deeper level than mere intellectual and academic consent***)*"* (Eph 4:23, Mirror Bible)

*"We stand fully identified in the new creation renewed in knowledge according to the pattern of the exact image of our creator."* (Col 3:10, Mirror Bible)

# *NINE*

## SONSHIP

*"Behold what manner of love the Father has bestowed on us, that we should be called children of God! Therefore the world does not know us, because it did not know Him. Beloved, now we are children of God; and it has not yet been revealed what we shall be, but we know that when He is revealed, we shall be like Him, for we shall see Him as He is."* (1 John 3:1-2).

We are the sons of God, we have become the sons of God through His love for us. It's a mystery to know how much God has valued us, revealing our true identity as sons. We compare ourselves with Old Testament prophets, we even desire to be like Moses, like Elijah, like David, we sing the songs of David and wish God could give a testimony of us just as He testified about David. We are still caught up in the old forgetting we are living in much better times than the prophets of old. They longed to live in these days, they longed for this intimacy we enjoy with God, we are like the prodigal son who wished he could be a servant in his father's house. We think what is true of the prophets is true of us. Listen child of God, what God has always known about us has finally been revealed, **you are not a second thought, you are the original idea God had.**

We are sons not born of flesh or the will of man but born from above. Flesh gives birth to flesh and Spirit gives birth to spirit,

(John 3:3-6). If my flesh ancestry was to be traced, it will lead back to Adam and should my spiritual origin be traced back it will lead back to Christ. That is where you have your spiritual ancestry. We carry a greater identity beyond our parents imagination, your conception could have been accidental to your parents but God knows your true identity and origin.

Every species gives birth after its kind, and God has given birth to us after His own kind. We carry the image and likeness of our Father God. *"Them that he called he also conformed to the image of His son"* (Rom 8:29), *"the spirit Himself bears witness with our spirit that we are the sons of God and He cries in us Abba Father."* (Rom 8:14-17). When Jesus was with His disciples He called them friends, He identified with them on a friendly basis but after the resurrection He appeared to Mary and said to her *"...but go to My brethren and say to them, 'I am ascending to My Father and your Father, and to My God and your God."* (John 20:17) After the resurrection, He calls them brothers no longer friends, the new birth has introduced sonship. We share the same Father and God with Jesus Christ.

## Adoption

Our understanding of adoption has robbed us of the blessing of sonship. Adoption in the Bible is not what we do in our tradition today. In our tradition, an adopted child does not carry the genetic detail of the parents who adopted them, this is not true to us. The word adoption is taken from the Jewish custom of adoption which was performed to every child who reached the age of inheriting. In the Jewish tradition, a father took his own child born to him and put him under tutors to train them the skills of life. When the child attained the age of maturity and was ready to be proclaimed an heir to the father, the father performed a special feast for the child, it was known as the adoption feast or *barmitsva* feast. *"Now I say that the heir, as long as he is a child, does not differ at all from a slave, though he is master of all, but is under guardians and stewards until the time appointed by the father."* (Gal 4:1-2)

On the said day, the father invited all his friends and relatives, he prepared a special coat for the son, it was known as a sonship coat, the father dressed his son in this special coat before the guests and proclaimed with a loud voice, 'this is my son' and from that moment the son was no longer a *'nepios'* (a child) but fully *"huios"* or *"kleronomos"* (son, an heir to the father). This is what was called the adoption feast. Paul compares this feast to our adoption as sons. *"Even so we, when we were children, were in bondage under the elements of the world. But when the fullness of the time had come, God sent forth His Son, born of a woman, born under the law, to redeem those who were under the law, that we might receive the adoption as sons. And because you are sons, God has sent forth the Spirit of His Son into your hearts, crying out, "Abba, Father!" Therefore you are no longer a slave but a son, and if a son, then an heir of God through Christ."* (Gal 4:3-7)

We were under bondage to the elements of this world, to the law, but the fullness of time has finally downed, we have gone through the adoption feast and the Spirit Himself cries Abba Father. *"But before faith came, we were kept under guard by the law, kept for the faith which would afterward be revealed. **Therefore the law*** *was our tutor to bring us to Christ, that we might be justified by faith. But after faith has come, we are no longer under a tutor. For you are all sons of God through faith in Christ Jesus. For as many of you as were baptized into Christ have put on Christ. There is neither Jew nor Greek, there is neither slave nor free, there is neither male nor female; for you are all one in Christ Jesus. And if you are Christ's, then you are Abraham's seed, and heirs according to the promise."* ( Gal 3:23-29). The law was our tutor and now faith has come, as many as have been baptized in to Christ have put on Christ, Christ is our sonship garment and the Spirit proclaims we are the sons of God.

The baptism of Jesus was symbolic to the adoption feast, any Jew who was conversant with the adoption feast realized what exactly took place during Jesus baptism. *"It came to pass in those days that Jesus came from Nazareth of Galilee, and was baptized by John in the Jordan. And immediately, coming up from the water, He saw the heavens parting and the Spirit descending upon Him like a dove. Then a voice came from heaven, "You are My beloved Son, in whom I am well pleased"* (Mark 1:9-11). After baptism Christ was clothed with power from above and a voice declared, *"you are my son in whom I am well pleased,"* this is what a father did to his son during the *Barmitsva* feast.

After this experience Jesus went into the wilderness and the devil come to tempt Him after forty days of prayer and fasting. The devil's question to Him was, *"if you are the son of God..."* he attacks His sonship, he makes Him doubt His sonship. That is the devil's game, He always targets to make us doubt our sonship.

## Likeness

We were not brought from a foreign country and made sons but born of the seed of God. Peter explains this to us *"your new life is not like your old life. Your old birth came from mortal sperm; your new birth comes from God's living Word. Just think: a life conceived by God himself!"* (1 Pet 1:23, Message). Wow, this translator brings it all out, have you ever imagined that you are conceived of God Himself, through God's living Word? God has produced after His own kind in you, you are the expression of the seed of God. His seed remains forever in you.

When you were physically conceived and born, you manifested the characteristics of your physical parents, you carried the seed of your parents, but now having been born of the seed of God, you can only manifest the characteristics of God. *"People conceived and brought into life by God don't make a practice of sin. How could they? God's seed is deep within them, making them who they are. It's not in the nature of the God-begotten to practice and parade sin."* (1 John 3:9, Message).

That's why Christ is not ashamed to call us His brothers, we have the same origin and have come from the same womb. The writer of Hebrews paints this picture to us. *"For both He who sanctifies and those who are sanctified are all from one Father; for which reason He is not ashamed to call them brethren, saying, "I WILL PROCLAIM YOUR NAME TO MY BRETHREN, IN THE MIDST OF THE CONGREGATION I WILL SING YOUR PRAISE." And again, "I WILL PUT MY TRUST IN HIM." And again, "BEHOLD, I AND THE*

*CHILDREN WHOM GOD HAS GIVEN ME.* " (Heb 2:11-13, NAS95) We are all of one Father, carrying the same seed of our Father; therefore He had to be made like His brothers in all aspects. He shared our life from the womb, birth to death. He tasted death like all of us and delivered us from the fear of death. We were associated in Him, the word association brings out a thought that God can not think of Christ at your exclusion. When one partner comes into God's mind the other also definitely comes in.

*"Because **God's children are human beings—made of flesh and blood—the Son also became flesh and blood.** For only as a human being could he die, and only by dying could he break the power of the devil, who had the power of death. Only in this way could he set free all who have lived their lives as slaves to the fear of dying. We also know that the Son did not come to help angels; he came to help the descendants of Abraham. Therefore, it was necessary **for him to be made in every respect like us, his brothers and sisters,** so that he could be our merciful and faithful High Priest before God. Then he could offer a sacrifice that would **take away the sins of the people**. Since he himself has gone through suffering and testing, he is able to help us when we are being tested. "* (Heb 2:14-18, NLT)

He was made like us in every respect, in every detail of human life. He become a merciful and faithful high priest before God. The good news is we have a human being representing us before God. Having tasted every detail of human life He can boldly present our issues before God, and offered a sacrifice that could take away our sins that we may share in His blameless life.

**Just as He was made like us in every detail, likewise we have been made like Him in every detail.** We share everything together, we share His righteousness, His love, His blameless life, His wisdom, His image and likeness, His peace and all that is true about Him is true in us. *"Again, a new commandment I write to you, which thing is true in Him and in you, because the darkness is passing away, and the true light is already shining."* (1 John 2:8). As He is so are we in this world, God sees us in the same capacity He see's Christ, God does not see you outside of Christ. What He sees in Christ is what He sees in us. **Christ is not the example for us to copy but the example of who we are.** As our brother, we share in the same characteristics.

*"He is the image of the invisible God, the firstborn over all creation."* (Col 1:15). Christ is the image of the invisible God, whatever is true in Him is true in us. *We are the image of the invisible God.* Whoever looks at us sees God. **Our lives are the best translation of the scripture,** the world should learn of God through our life just as it was at the church in Antioch. See how this translation puts it, *"We look at this Son and see the God who cannot be seen. We look at this Son and see God's original purpose in everything created."* (Message)

*"For it pleased the Father that in Him all the fullness should dwell"* (Col 1:19). In Christ all the fullness of God dwells bodily. That which is true in Him is equally true in us, *all the fullness of*

**God dwells in us.** "*So spacious is he, so roomy, that everything of God finds its proper place in him without crowding.*" (Message) Paul tells the Ephesians they should be filled with all the fullness of God. "*Live full lives, full in the fullness of God.*" (Eph 3:19, Message).

"*Yet now he has reconciled you to himself through the death of Christ in his physical body. As a result, he has brought you into his own presence, and you are holy and blameless as you stand before him without a single fault.*" (Col 1:22, NLT). As He is so are we, **holy and blameless without fault before Him.** God can not see you outside of Christ. "*He accomplished this in dying our death in a human body, He fully represented us in order to fully present us again in blameless innocence, face to face with God; with no sense of guilt, suspicion, regret or accusation; all charges against us are officially cancelled.*" (Mirror Bible)

"*In whom are hidden all the treasures of wisdom and knowledge.*" (Col 2:3). All treasure of wisdom and knowledge are locked up in Christ, as He is so are we in this world. *All treasure of wisdom and knowledge are locked up in us by the Spirit of God.* We have received the mind of Christ. "*For "who has known the mind of the LORD that he may instruct Him?" But we have the mind of Christ.*" (1 Cor 2:16). We have received the mind of Christ and the Spirit of Christ.

"*But you've seen and heard it because God by his Spirit has brought it all out into the open before you. The Spirit, not content to flit around on the surface, dives into the depths of God, and brings out what God planned all along. Whoever knows what you're thinking and planning except you yourself? The same with God—except that he not only knows what he's thinking, but he lets us in on it. God offers a full report on the gifts of life and salvation that he is giving us. We don't have to rely on the world's guesses and opinions. We didn't learn this by reading books or going to school; we learned it from God, who taught us person-to-person through Jesus, and we're passing it on to you in the same firsthand, personal way, ... ... Spiritually alive, we have access to everything God's Spirit is doing, and can't be judged by unspiritual critics. Isaiah's question, "Is there anyone around who knows God's Spirit, anyone who knows what he is doing?" has been answered: Christ knows, and we have Christ's Spirit. "* (1 Cor 2:10-13, 15-16. Message)

*"I and my Father are one. "* (John 10:30). Christ and the Father are one, whatever is true in Him is equally true in us, *we are one with the father. "that they all may be one, as You, Father, are in Me, and I in You; that they also may be one in Us, that the world may believe that You sent Me. "I in them, and You in Me; that they may be made perfect in one, and that the world may know that You have sent Me, and have loved them as You have loved Me. "* (John 17:21, 23). Our union with Him is what God intended from the beginning that man will not be separate from God. As the Father loves Christ so does He love us, brothers from the same womb.

*"Most assuredly, I say to you, he who believes in Me, the works that I do he will do also; and greater works than these he will do, because I go to My Father. "* (John 14:12). **The works He did He**

*promised we shall also do the same and more than that* because whatever is true in Him is equally true in us. *"For we are God's fellow workers"* (1 Cor 3:9). As He is so are we in this world. *"And as we live in God, our love grows more perfect. So we will not be afraid on the day of judgment, but we can face him with confidence because we live like Jesus here in this world."* (1 John 4:17, NLT)

To arm yourself with this understanding of how complete you are in Christ and how God sees you will liberate you from trying to become what already you are. It will help you to manifest what you already are and your prayer will change from asking God to give you more and more, to thanking God for the much He has already delivered to us. With this understanding it will be easy to manifest what you already have. God has done it all. Stop entertaining religion which always likes to postpone even what is already done. Paul the apostle paints a clear picture to us about all that has already happened in his writing to the church in Ephesus. He prays for the believers in Ephesus not to be given something new from heaven but that the eyes of their understanding may be enlightened to see.( Eph 1:18).

Christianity is not a life of people who need things from God but a life of those who have discovered how much they have already received in Christ. As the sons of God, He has given us all, we have the privilege of enjoying what has freely been given to us. The Spirit of God reveals to us the things we have freely received from our Father. Unfortunately we still labor trying to get what has been freely delivered to us. Righteousness, holiness, peace, comfort, blessings, forgiveness have been given to us free. "Love, joy, peace are not fragile fading emotions, produced by will power. They are the fruit of what you know in your spirit to be true about you," [1] says Francois du Toit. *"Let the communication of your faith endeavor to the discovery of every good thing that is in you in Christ Jesus."* (Philemon 6). God's desire is to reveal within you a treasure of immeasurable wealth. A wealth that surpasses all prayer requests. Nothing will please you more than to know and believe the true testimony of you, this is the most attractive life you can live conscious of. No amount of prayer or fasting could add to the mineral wealth that is already deposited in the earth, all is in place waiting to be discovered and explored. Discover and explore what is in you.

We have the mind of Christ (1 Cor 2:16), that's why none can judge you because they can not judge God. As God calls things which are not as though they are so we should do the same. Don't judge life through circumstances, *"we have the same Spirit of faith as it is written "I believed so I spoke", so do we believe and speak."* (2 Cor 4:13). There is nothing God has hidden from us as His sons, In Matt 13:11, Jesus declares to His disciples it has been given to them the right to know the secrets of God. We have access as sons into the wisdom of God but we fail to use it. It's like buying an expensive phone with many features for your grand mother who does not understand the use of internet, WI-FI or blue-tooth but boasts of having an expensive phone.

"Nothing makes you vulnerable than to be driven by a sense of need and lack, **nothing makes you more beautiful and**

**confident than a sense of total fulfillment**. The most profound and significant virtue of man is the capacity of the individual to comprehend and reflect the impression, image and likeness of God. Your greatest feature is His glory (doxa - opinion) His opinion reflecting in you. This persuasion becomes an awareness within you which makes your life irresistibly attractive[1]."

1. *Francois du Toit. God believes in you.* pg 28

202

# TEN

## VALUE

Thank God that you have come this far with me, by now I guess you have learnt alot. I invite you to join me again as we discover the value that God has placed in each and every individual. On many occasions the Pharisees and the Sadducees complained of Jesus association with sinners and Jesus sought to give them a good answer. Does it not surprise us that sinners were the companions of Christ, but today the so called 'sinners' fear stepping on the doors of our churches?

Jesus at no time rebuked sinners but rebuked hypocrisy and unbelief which we entertain today. He was labeled a friend of sinners by the pharisees and scribes. God's grace carries the answer to sinners. Grace removes condemnation and sets us free from sin. He first removed condemnation from the woman caught in adultery (John 8) and told her not to sin, but we condemn people and ask them not to sin.

*"Then all the tax collectors and the sinners drew near to Him to hear Him. And the Pharisees and scribes complained, saying, "This Man receives sinners and eats with them." So He spoke this parable to them, saying: "What man of you, having a hundred sheep, if he loses one of them, does not leave the ninety–nine in the wilderness, and go after the one which is lost until he finds it? "And when he has found it, he lays it on his shoulders, rejoicing.*

*"And when he comes home, he calls together his friends and neighbors, saying to them, 'Rejoice with me, for I have found my sheep which was lost!'*

*"I say to you that likewise there will be more joy in heaven over one sinner who repents than over ninety–nine just persons who need no repentance. "Or what woman, having ten silver coins, if she loses one coin, does not light a lamp, sweep the house, and search carefully until she finds it? "And when she has found it, she calls her friends and neighbors together, saying, 'Rejoice with me, for I have found the piece which I lost!' "Likewise, I say to you, there is joy in the presence of the angels of God over one sinner who repents. "* (Luke 15:1-10)

**Lost Sheep.**

The Pharisees complained and Jesus answers them through this parable. This issue was so dear to Jesus that He had to use three parables to answer it. **The lost sheep did not loose it's value**, it's value remained intact. The unbeliever has not lost value, God sees value in each one of us which can not be eroded by sin. Man lived in sin for long but sin did not erode the value of any single individual. The fact that the sheep was lost only implies it had an owner, it only went out of the owners sight but it was still in the owners mind. Man has always been in God's mind, the owner had never given up on it and went out to recover that which belonged to him.

Man has never been and will never be a property of the devil. A thief may steal something and keep it for as long as he could but it will never be his, when the police catch up with him, he will be arrested for handling stolen property. The thief come to kill, steal and destroy but the owner has finally come that we may have life and life in abundance, (John 10:10). At one moment the Pharisees threatened to kill Jesus, (John 8:44). He referred to them as being of the devil their father, He meant the ideologies they carried belonged to the devil not from God. In the next two chapters He quotes from the Psalm of Asaph (Ps 82:6), where it says *"ye are gods and the sons of the most high."* (John 10:34). They belonged to God but they were carrying the devils ideologies. **Our religion today has handed over the mass of mankind to the devil on a silver platter**. We say all unbelievers are of the devil, the devil owns no human life and the right owner has laid down His life and redeemed that which belongs to Him.

When the owner found the lost sheep, he called all his friends to celebrate with him. Jesus says this is the joy of the heavens over one sinner who repents, who changes his mind; there is celebration in heaven over one more life discovering its value and being restored to the original owner.

## Lost Coin

Which woman having ten coins and loses one does not light a lamp, sweeps the house and search carefully until she finds the coin? The lost coin never loses value. One time while walking on a lonely street I bounced on some money which accidentally somebody had lost. That money could buy anything of that amount, it never lost its value because it was lost from the owner.

The inscription on that coin makes it a legal tender recognized by the central bank. The image of God in the human spirit is in much the same way preserved like a water mark on a paper note. When Jesus was challenged by the Pharisees if they should pay taxes, He lifted up a coin and asked them whose image and inscription was on the coin. He could as well have lifted up a human being and asked them whose image and likeness was he bearing. Return to God what belongs to God. The lost coin had its owner only that she couldn't see it but it was still in her mind. She had not forgotten about it, you can't lose what does not belong to you. The word lost communicates ownership.

She lights a lamp. *"Then Jesus spoke to them again, saying, "I am the light of the world. He who follows Me shall not walk in darkness, but have the light of life."* (John 8:12). Jesus is our light. Light reveals that which darkness hides. Darkness is not a force but the absence of light, when light shines there is no contention, darkness gives way. **Man can only discover his value in the light of what God says and did**. The word of God lights our paths and our lives, it reveals to us who we are, who God is and what God has done for us and in us. We can only know our true identity in His word. *"For you are the fountain of life, the light by which we see."* (Psalms 36:9, NLT) Only in His light can we see or else darkness (ignorance) will always blind our understanding and fail to realize what God has done for us.

That is what the devil prides in doing, He has blinded (darkened) the minds of the unbelievers that they should not see the light of the gospel of the glory of Jesus Christ who is the image of the invisible God, (2 Cor 4:4). He has filled their minds with unbelief but the gospel lights their understanding and fills them with the knowledge of who they are. This light shines in us, *"For God, who said, "Let there be light in the darkness," has made this light shine in our hearts so we could know the glory of God that is seen in the face of Jesus Christ."* (Vs 6, NLT). The same glory of God in the face of Jesus Christ is the same glory that is revealed in us. This glory (Doxa- opinion) is the knowledge of God, what God says about us and Has revealed about us through Jesus Christ. Jesus Christ is God's glory (opinion) about us. The word of God reveals the glory of God which lights our lives and brings transformation in the spirit of our minds. Light creates nothing new, it illuminates what already exists, it helps you see the complete you.

She sweeps the house and searches carefully till she finds the coin. The coin was not lost far from the owner, it was lost in her house. The world and its fullness belongs to God, man has not been lost in a foreign planet which his maker does not own but man has always been in the vicinity of his creator. Sin hindered us from seeing the value in us. Just as this woman had to sweep the house and remove the dirt which concealed the coin, God had to deal with sin which concealed the value of each and every individual. **Sin did not reduce the value of man but hid that which was true about us**. Christ came to seek and save that which was lost and now that which has been found is not to be lost.

She searched every place where the coin could have been hid until she found it. God did everything to rescue us back to Himself. He removed every obstacle that stood before us so that we could discover our true identity. When she found the coin she called her friends to celebrate with her. God rejoices over every individual who discovers his true self and turns to God.

## Lost Son

*Then He said: "A certain man had two sons. "And the younger of them said to his father, 'Father, give me the portion of goods that falls to me.' So he divided to them his livelihood. "And not many days after, the younger son gathered all together, journeyed to a far country, and there wasted his possessions with prodigal living. "But when he had spent all, there arose a severe famine in that land, and he began to be in want. "Then he went and joined himself to a citizen of that country, and he sent him into his fields to feed swine. "And he would gladly have filled his stomach with the pods that the swine ate, and no one gave him anything. "But when he came to himself, he said, 'How many of my father's hired servants have bread enough and to spare, and I perish with hunger! 'I will arise and go to my father, and will say to him, "Father, I have sinned against heaven and before you, "and I am no longer worthy to be called your son. Make me like one of your hired servants. "*

*"And he arose and came to his father. But when he was still a great way off, his father saw him and had compassion, and ran and fell on his neck and kissed him. "And the son said to him, 'Father, I have sinned against heaven and in your sight, and am no longer worthy to be called your son.' "But the father said to his servants, 'Bring out the best robe and put it on him, and put a ring*

*on his hand and sandals on his feet. 'And bring the fatted calf here and kill it, and let us eat and be merry; 'for this my son was dead and is alive again; he was lost and is found.' And they began to be merry."* (Luke 15:11-24)

Remember Jesus is still addressing the Pharisees who complained about His involvement with sinners. The father had two sons who both had reached the age of inheritance. The younger son asks for what belonged to Him. There is something which always belongs to you and the Father knows that well. The father divided to them His livelihood and the younger son took what belonged to him and left for a far country, far from his father and his family, he spent all he had and finally was in want. He found a job of feeding pigs. Get it well, Jesus is addressing Pharisees and scribes who clearly understood what feeding pigs meant. According to the law of Moses, pigs were unclean animals and Jews could not associate with pigs. It represented sinful life. He even desired to eat the pods which the swine ate but no one gave him, he almost become a pig.

The son came to himself, he decided in his mind he will go back home to his father and ask the father to forgive him and make him like one of the servants. While he was still a great way off, his father who had always been longing and missing his son saw him, he ran to meet him, kissed and hugged him without asking him questions where he had been or what he had done with his money or how he had spent his livelihood. The legalistic Pharisees must have raised their eyebrows when they heard how the father received the son who was involved with feeding the swine. The son was unclean and definitely when the father hugged him he also shared in his uncleanness. The father did not listen to the confession (mentioning his sins) of the son, he was busy asking the servants to cloth the son with the best robe he had kept for the son, to put a ring in his finger and nice shoes to his feet and prepare a feast to celebrate his son's return. That is the nature of our Father, He is waiting for your return, He misses you with a passion. Sin could not prevent Him from loving man, He has always and will always love you, He fully identified with our sinful status.

## Guilt and Condemnation.

We always ask when did this son repent? How comes the father never listened to his confession? When the son came to himself and decided to go back to the father that was the true repentance. He changed his mind and saw it worthy to go back home. When the father saw him He knew the boy had a change of mind that's why he was back home. Guilt and condemnation had put the son down, he came feeling guilty and condemned in his mind that's why he prepared a confession of sin to see if the father would forgive him and accept him.

The father did not entertain his guilt and did not condemn him, this is our Father's attitude, He does not condemn us for our sins, He has no time to entertain our guilt, He sees value in us. What God wants is for us to have a change of mind, to align our thoughts with His thoughts. The son thought sin had reduced him from being a son into being a servant, he pleaded with the father to make him a servant. That's what guilt does to us believers, it reduces us to what we are not, we see ourselves as sinners and yet the Father sees us as saints, we plead with God to restore us yet the father sees sons. Remember God sees us as He sees Christ, as Christ is so are we in this world, if Christ is blameless so are you. The father knew nothing could reduce the value he had placed on his son, **the son who left and the son who stayed home had the same value.**

Sometime I wonder why God could not have delayed the coming of Jesus to the 20th century or 21st century when man had some technological advancement. Christ could have done His ministry on live television and reached so many people, we could have sold television rights to make money for His ministry. God saw value in man that He could not wait for technology. All technology put together can not equal the value of one individual. Technology has kept advancing year after year, the phone you bought last year is completely irrelevant today in comparison with the latest phone in the market. Does it not surprise you that since Adam, God has not improved on the human race? Neither has He added more minerals on earth? God did a complete work and He rested, His work does not need improvement (Ecc 3:14).

Do not entertain guilt in your life, this is a weapon the devil uses more effectively and it always makes you more vulnerable to commit other sins. You feel you are not worthy because of what has happened, you are filled with anger why did it happen, and become so bitter with people and angry at yourself. You even fear talking to God; you feel you are a disappointment to God. When it comes to this you are playing in the league the devil has always wished and he will keep reminding you of the mistake you did so that you can continue in this state. Guilt will always drive you from the Father and the brothers.

Thank God He does not entertain our pity parties but religion enjoys this, religion would always want you to feel guilty so that you can always spend your life in cycles of asking for forgiveness everyday. The father did not condemn him for anything he had done, he was not interested in his story, he knew his son was lost and now is found, was dead and now is alive. That is the joy of your Father. He ordered the robe of sonship and the ring of authority and shoes to be restored to his son. He killed the fattened calf to celebrate the return of his son. God rejoices over any soul that repents and discovers their true identity.

## Religion and Tradition

*"Now his older son was in the field. And as he came and drew near to the house, he heard music and dancing. "So he called one of the servants and asked what these things meant. "And he said to him, 'Your brother has come, and because he has received him safe and sound, your father has killed the fatted calf.' "But he was angry and would not go in. Therefore his father came out and pleaded with him. "So he answered and said to his father, 'Lo, these many years I have been serving you; I never transgressed your commandment at any time; and yet you never gave me a young goat, that I might make merry with my friends. 'But as soon as this son of yours came, who has devoured your livelihood with harlots, you killed the fatted calf for him.' "And he said to him,*

*'Son, you are always with me, and all that I have is yours. 'It was right that we should make merry and be glad, for your brother was dead and is alive again, and was lost and is found."* (Luke 15:25-32)

When the elder brother came home and heard the sound of music and celebration at home, he was surprised. Since his brother had left there had been no celebration or music at home. He asked one of the servants what all this meant and was told your brother is home. I thought this elder son should have been happy to receive his brother back home, he should have rushed to the house just to kiss his brother to know how life is out there but that was not the case, he was angry and could not go in.

Brothers we have not taken serious the issue of having our brothers back home. We have never put on the passion of reaching out to the lost and bringing them home with a dance, we have never missed them enough to go for them. This is a call to you and me, there is a brother out there who should be home, let's get them home, and let's celebrate their return. We were all sons in Adam from the beginning (Luke 3:38). Our elder brother Jesus took it upon Himself to bring us home, He came to seek and save us.

When the father heard that his elder son was out there refusing to come in, he never sent a servant to bring him home but he took it upon himself with the same determination to bring the elder son home. **It is not us who go to Him but He is always there for us in every situation of life**. When you feel discouraged and broken, you will always hear a voice strengthening you, He is always beside us and with us in every situation of life. The son says how many years he has served the father. He served to catch the father's attention that he may reward him. Your service does not make you more of a son than already you are. The Father has always had your attention, no amount of service will change this fact. There are many of us who exhaust ourselves and go to greater heights trying to catch God's attention. God's eyes and ears have always and will always be inclined to you. Let our service to God be out of gratitude and also a sense of responsibility, out of joy as sons in the house, let it not be trying to change God's mind about you. God's mind about us was made up long time when He came for us. Jesus portrayed the mind of God about us.

The son says he has not transgressed any commandment of the father. He reduced his relationship to the father to the level of keeping commands like a servant. **Sonship is not about keeping rules but a relationship,** how we relate to the Father. Many of us today think God hears us because we keep the commandments, God does not relate to us on the basis of how many commandments we have kept but on the basis of being a son. Keeping commandments or not does not make you to be more or less of a son neither does it make you earn God's favor. Religion and tradition have made us believe we have fellowship with God on the basis of keeping commandments and service to God. Rules are given to children, but sons have grown passed the age of being given rules. Christ has made us sons and took us from the level of keeping rules to being heirs of God and joint heirs with Christ

Jesus. Those who still live under rules are in the elementary principles, they are unskilled in the word of righteousness that's why they still believe they have to perform to be righteous, they are still babes using milk. They don't know how to differentiate good from evil, that's why they need rules to order them around, (Heb 5:13-14). Look here, one son is at home and behaves like a servant and another son is out there longing to come home and be a servant. None of these sons understood there relationship with their father.

My son does not relate to me on the basis of keeping rules, he enjoys doing what pleases the father because he enjoys the relationship. This son wanted the father to kill a young goat for him and his friends and yet all that was left belonged to him. The father had divided his wealth among the two and according to the Jewish tradition the elder son received double. All belonged to him yet he never killed even a young goat to enjoy with his friends. He was busy serving like a servant yet he was the owner.

The irony of this story is that the son was busy working in the fields while the servants were at home enjoying the fellowship of the father. He was so busy for the kingdom and the father was left home lonely, longing for fellowship. No wander the father felt great when his other son came back. How often do we serve to get what has already been given to us, Many believers who have the Spirit of God still struggle with things which have been freely given to them, that is exactly why the Spirit lives in us to make us know what we have freely received. We give curse breaking offerings, we pay for special prayers, carrying anointing oil everywhere as our security and many more, all has been given to you already in Christ. It's about discovering what belongs to you and taking it, this elder son never knew what belonged to him.

"As soon as this son of yours came," he excludes himself from sonship, he does not say 'as soon as his brother came' but this son of yours. He even suggests this younger son had devoured his living with prostitutes. He says he has 'devoured your livelihood.' Whatever God gives to you is yours not His anymore. You can bless somebody if you wish, give it to church or do what you wish with it. God never gives you anything and withholds it back, that does not foster generosity. Could it be possible he knew where his brother was but failed to go for him? This son suffered from recognition, he desired to be recognized by the father, what was wrong by the father killing a calf? Nothing, he only desired it could have been killed for him.

He fell into self pity and yet all these were at his disposal. The father calls him "child," he was a son behaving like a child. *"You are always with me and all that is mine is yours."* We haven't known that we are always with Him, He promised never to leave us or forsake us unconditionally, He never leaves us and comes back when we pray, no, He is always with us. *"All that is of the Father belongs to the Son and when the Spirit of God comes He will take that which belongs to the Son and declare it to us,"* (John 16:15) that was the promise of Jesus to us. Your brother was lost and now is found was dead and now is a live. We are not told if the elder son came in or if he remained outside. It's a call to believers to lay down the cards of performance and approach God on the basis of sonship and fellowship, not boasting of what we have done. Christianity is not a test to perform, it is a rest. Enjoy the sabbath rest.

When one sheep out of a hundred was lost the shepherd never dismissed it because it was just one, when one coin out of ten was lost the woman never gave up on it, and when one son out of two disappeared the father never gave up on him. The sheep illustrates one percent of the sheep, the coin was ten percent of the entire amount and the son was fifty percent of the sons. In all the cases the owners were very much involved and concerned. It simply means if only one soul was lost out of the seven billion souls in the world today, the good shepherd could have still come for that one soul. And if six billion out of the seven billion souls were lost the good shepherd could still have come for them. *"(God) who is willing for all mankind to be saved and come to a full knowledge of the truth."* (2 Tim 2:4, Weymouth).

**Favor Not Labor**
The parable ends without us knowing if the son went in or never went in. The invitation still remains for many of us out there who are sons but are behaving like servants, God has come to bring you to enjoy sonship and not servant-hood. You can enter the rest of God and cease from your religious labor of trying to earn God's favor by your performance. God wants to relate to you on the basis of what Christ has done and not what you have done. It is always a tendency of man to feel he has played a part in all that God does. You will hear many people giving testimonies how God blessed them because they planted seeds, they prayed, they

fasted, they went to church and so much more. What they do, only raises their expectations and that makes them to receive. God wants to bless you not out of your labor but out of His favor. *"When people work, their wages are not a gift, but something they have earned,"* (Rom 4:4, NLT).

Your provision is not based on how much seed you have sown but on your value as a son, **it is not work based but worth based**. Jesus said we are of more value than the birds of the air which do not sow nor reap but are fed every day (Matt 6:26, 30). Look, birds don't know the principle of sowing and reaping yet they eat and drink, to rely on principles is to lower yourself to a lower realm of provision, your provision is worth based not work based as a son. Sowing and reaping is an earthly principle (Gen 8:22). God meets your needs according to His riches in Glory in Christ, not the seeds we've sown. He was rich yet for your sake He become poor that you through His poverty may become rich. That is the basis of your prosperity which the Corinthian believers knew and walked in. They enjoyed God's prosperity because of this. (2 Cor 8:9)

God tells Abraham in (Gen 22:1-), give me your only son, God knew very well Abraham had two sons, Ishmael and Isaac, Ishmael was a product of Abrahams own effort to help God, Isaac was the son of promise born of God's will. God does not recognize anything born out of will power and not His power, you can have the biggest congregation and hold big crusades but if it's out of your will power and not God, it's not counted by God. Performance has no basis in this, Paul says the grace of God worked in him, (1Cor 15:10).

He did enough in Christ to warrant you to rest and enjoy His blessings in your life. Adam's first day on earth was God's resting day. He welcomed Adam into a life of rest because He did every thing for man's survival. This does not mean that we should not pray or go to church, no. Our motivation to pray or go to church should not be to earn God's favor, or God's blessings, Let your prayer be motivated by a sense of gratitude, fulfillment and relationship to God. Let it be out of a sense of appreciation to what God has done for us not a duty which when you fail to honor you will be subjected to punishment. God is out to relate with us as sons, co-workers and coheirs with Jesus Christ. We should not pray to be loved by God but our praying will make us love God more, our giving will help us love God more, our going to church will help us love God more.

Isaiah 54 is so much familiar to us, we say no weapon fashioned against us will succeed in Vs 17. Isaiah 54 comes after 53, In 53, Isaiah speaks of the sufferings of Christ, the price He paid that we should enjoy every blessing written in 54. Isaiah 53 speaks of the rejection He went through, chastisement for our peace, afflicted, wounded, stripped for our healing, oppression, sorrow and grief, stricken for transgression. He went through all this that we should enjoy the fruit of it all. "*He shall see the fruit the travail of his soul and shall be satisfied....*" (Isa 53:11, RSV)

God feels happy when we enjoy the product of His travail. Isaiah 54 speaks of fruitfulness, enlargement, shame removed, companionship with God, never to forsake us. He promises never to be angry with you nor rebuke you again because His anger against sin was absorbed on Christ's body. He was chastised on my behalf. He has made an everlasting covenant of love and peace with us, no more enmity, He promises wealth, peace and prosperity for our children, He promises establishment and no oppression upon us. And finally He speaks of the famous one, no weapon fashioned against us will prevail. God delights to see all these manifested in our lives and we enjoy them because He gave out His soul for these. He purchased all for you and for me. Christ worked on our behalf and now He calls us into His rest, everything has been worked on at the cross, the quarry, yours is to enjoy the product of the cross.

This parable also paints to us a picture of grace and law. The younger son represents the gentiles who are restored to God by grace. We never deserved the favor of God but by His love and grace, He received us and embraced us and restored us into sonship as it was in Adam. The elder son represents the Jewish nation which embraced the law and related to God on the basis of the law. They missed a relationship with God because of their preoccupation with the law. They failed to enjoy God's blessing because of the demands of the law.

We thank God for having revealed to us His intended purpose for man. This book is written that we may enjoy the loving relationship with our God not to be bound by the religious principles which have stolen joy and life from us. It is a call to the church to get out of the box, the traditions which the church has embraced which are not in line with God's will for us. Enjoy the freedom that God has called us into and be not bound by any yoke of slavery to traditions and religion.

As you peer into these truths with the keenness and clear vision as of an eagle, you will see as God sees and believe what God believes. This material is meant to help you walk in what has freely been given to us. A life that flows from God and has no struggles but effortlessly manifests through us. When you take something that is supposed to be a fruit and make it a command you turn it into a law and you will not experience its blessing but will be a burden to you. This is the truth about the reality of the gospel. Diamond discovered did not become diamond on the day it was discovered, no it was always diamond and always there but hidden from men. There are many who died poor and were buried on top of those mines but their lives were not changed. The discovery of these diamonds is what makes the difference. Discover truth and walk in it.

**Life can be experienced on one of two levels, the reward or the gift principle.** The reward principle will always be predictable and consistent with personal effort and achievement, whereas the gift dimension opens opportunity beyond any limitations to personal credit. The gift principle is what God intended for you to walk and enjoy life which has been paid for and given to us, says Francois du Toit.

I believe this material has blessed your life just as it has been a blessing to me, I welcome you to get involved in enjoying this effortless life God has given us and you will not struggle in life.

We have used different translations to bring out the truth. When King James Version was written in 1611, the translators quoted

Augustine as proof "that variety of translation is profitable for the finding out the sense of the scripture."[1] So even the translators of King James new the importance of other translations.

Should you wish to write to me to give a testimony of what God has done to you through this revelation, feel free, and should you wish to support us spread this message feel free.

Bonface Odhiambo
P. O. Box 28831 Code 00200
Nairobi, Kenya.

Contact me through this e-mail.
bonfireod@gmail.com

For more grace resources, audio, video and print materials visit

us on.
Website: www.gracefamilychapel.net

Abbreviations.

AV......................Authorised Version

ISV.....................International Standard Version

Message.............The Message Bible (Colorado Springs: NavPress Publishing
Group, 2007 ed,). by Eugene Peterson-2007

Mirror................Mirror Bible Translation. Visit (www.mirrorword.net)
Francois du Toit

NAS...................New American Standard Version.

NAS95 ..............1995 New American Standard (Version La Habra, Ca.: The
Lockman Foundation, 1977, 1995)

NKJV ................New King James Version (Thomas Nelson Publishers, 1982)

NLT...................New Living Translation (Wheaton: Tyndale House
Publishers, 1996, 2004, 2007).

NRSV ............... 1989 New Revised Standard Version

RSV.................1947The Holy Bible Revised Standard Version.
(New York: Thomas Nelson & Sons, 1947)

WEY..................1912 Weymouth NT. Translation (The new Testament in
modern speech, Richard Francis Weymouth)

YLT.................... Young's Literal Translation

www.ingramcontent.com/pod-product-compliance
Lightning Source LLC
Chambersburg PA
CBHW051953090426
42741CB00008B/1380